Churchill's Bunker

ALSO BY RICHARD HOLMES

In order of publication

The English Civil War (with Brigadier Peter Young)

The Little Field Marshal: Sir John French

Soldiers (with John Keegan)

Firing Line

The Road to Sedan

Fatal Avenue

Riding the Retreat

War Walks

War Walks II

The Western Front

The Second World War in Photographs

The First World War in Photographs

Oxford Companion to Military History (general editor)

Battlefields of the Second World War

Redcoat: The British Soldier in the Age of Horse and Musket

Wellington: The Iron Duke

Tommy: The British Soldier on the Western Front, 1914–1918

In the Footsteps of Churchill

Sahib: The British Soldier in India

Dusty Warriors: Modern Soldiers at War

The World at War

Marlborough: England's Fragile Genius

Shots from the Front

Churchill's Bunker

The Cabinet War Rooms and the Culture of Secrecy in Wartime London

RICHARD HOLMES

Yale
UNIVERSITY PRESS
NEW HAVEN & LONDON

First published in the United States in 2010 by Yale University Press.
First published in Great Britain in 2009 by Profile Books Ltd. in
association with the Imperial War Museum.

Typeset in Swift by MacGuru Ltd.
Printed in the United States of America.

Library of Congress Control Number: 2009938871
ISBN 978-0-300-16040-6 (hardcover : alk. paper)

A catalogue record for this book is available from the British Library.

This paper meets the requirements of ANSI/NISO Z39.48-1992
(Permanence of Paper).

10 9 8 7 6 5 4 3 2 1

CONTENTS

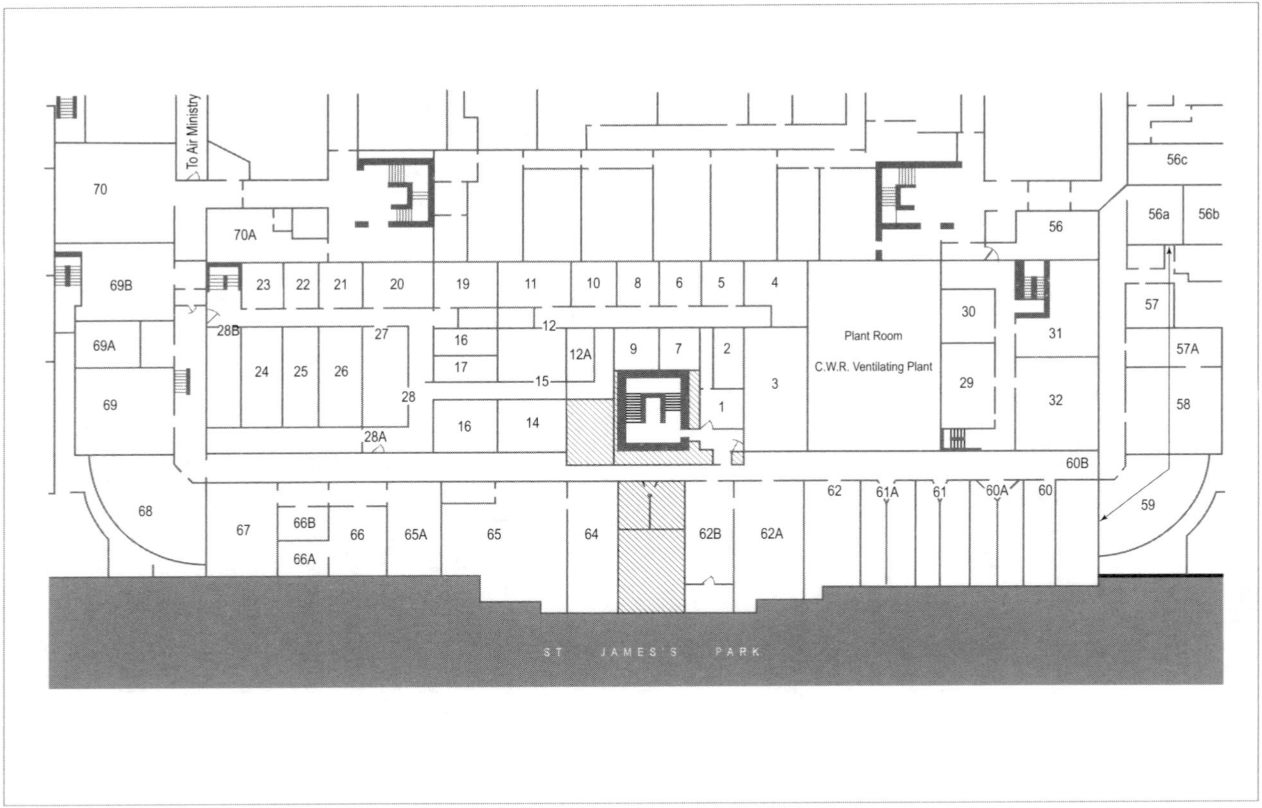
To Air Ministry
70
70A
69B
69A
69
68
23
22
21
20
19
11
10
8
6
5
4
28B
27
24
25
26
28
28A
16
17
12
15
12A
9
7
2
1
3
16
14
Plant Room
C.W.R. Ventilating Plant
30
29
56
31
32
60B
67
66B
66A
66
65A
65
64
62B
62A
62
61A
61
60A
60
56c
56a
56b
57
57A
58
59
ST JAMES'S PARK

Plan of the Cabinet War Rooms basement, circa 1944

1	Butler's pantry and kitchen
2	Mrs Churchill, 1 bed
3	Chiefs of Staff (COS)
4	Minister of Labour, 1 bed
5	Lt Col King-Salter, 1 bed
6	Commander Thompson, 1 bed
7	PM's dining room
8	Major Morton, 1 bed
9	Mr Brendan Bracken, 1 bed
10	Brig Harvie-Watt, 1 bed
11	Miss Stenhouse's section
12	Doorway to PM's typing pool
12A	PM's detectives, 2 beds
13	Not shown
14	Cleaning gear
15	Doorway to PM's typing pool
16	Lord Woolton, 1 bed
17	Mr Anthony Eden, 1 bed
18	Mr Clement Attlee, 1 bed
19	Sir John Anderson, 1 bed
20	Mr Murrie
21	Brig Jacob
22	Colonel Price
23	Lt Col Oliver
24	Group Capt Earle, Capt Oswald, Mr Beer, Mrs Noble
25	Miss Gray, Miss Cooper, Miss Bright, Miss Spearing, Miss Bright, Miss Lewis, Mrs Roberts
26	Miss Fairlie, Miss Tower, Miss Bacchus – Typists section, A&B (COS)
27	Defence Registry
28	COS clerks
28A	RM's N0.10 Annexe
28B	Mrs Hill, Miss Leyton, Miss Hamblin
29	Canteen
30	First Aid
31	Telephonists' rest room
32	Telephone exchange
33–55	Not shown
56A	Joint planners
56B	Joint planners
56C	Administrative
57	Special accommodation
57A	Special accommodation
58	Special accommodation
59	Special accommodation
60	Left: PM's PBX, BBC equipment Right: Mr Winnifrith
60A	Left: Sir Gilbert Laithwaite,1 bed Right: Lt. Col. Capel-Dunn,1 bed
61	Left: Lt. Col. McEwan, 2 bunks Right: Gen. Ismay, 1 bed
61A	Left: Mr Armstrong, Mr Blaker,1 bed Right: Sir E Bridges, 1 bed
62	Miss Fyfe, Miss Macaulay, Miss Gill, Miss Lindars, Miss Aithie, Miss Green, Miss Brown, Miss Arnold, 3 beds
62A	Royal Marines Mess room, 1 bed
62B	Mr Burgis, Major Rawlings, Mr Walter, 1 bed
64	Lt Col Weber-Brown, Map room annexe
65	Map room
65A	PM, 1 bed
66	2 PM's PS, 2 beds
66B	Mr Martin
66A	1PM's PS, 1 bed
67	PM's private office
68	PM's waiting room
69	Cabinet room
69A	Major-General Hollis, 1 bed: outer office Mr James, Miss Le Sueur
69B	Emergency Lavatories
70	Unknown
70A	Unknown

Note: Reconstructed from a blurred original in the Churchill Museum. Some names are speculative, others remain elusive.

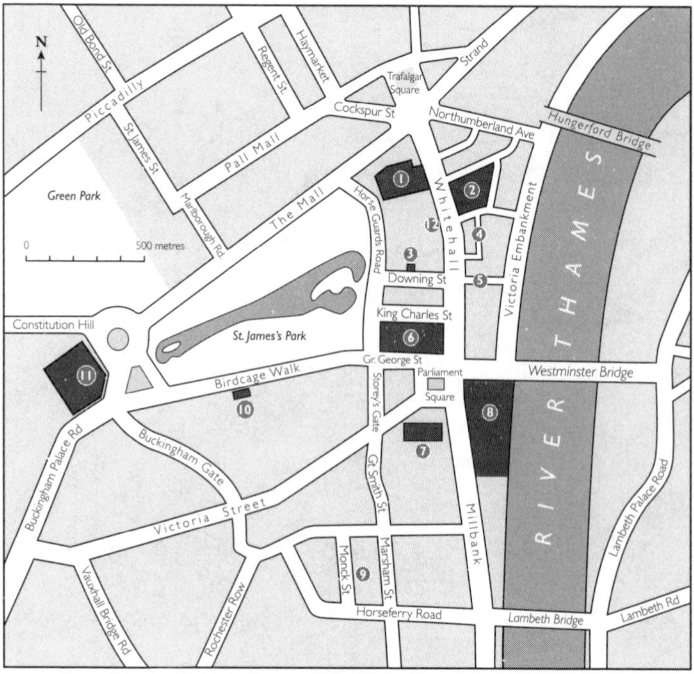

1 Admiralty
2 War Office
3 No. 10 Downing Street
4 Whitehall Gardens
5 Richmond Terrace
6 New Public Offices
7 Westminster Abbey
8 Houses of Parliament
9 'Anson'
10 Guards Chapel
11 Buckingham Palace
12 Horse Guards

FOREWORD

When Winston Churchill said that, in war, 'you have to run risks', one cannot help but wonder if he knew the degree of risk he ran in meeting in a poorly converted, poorly reinforced and poorly sited storage basement in Whitehall during the heaviest enemy bombing raids on London. Certainly, the few hundred people whose wartime lives were very largely spent in this secret complex felt secure there, even though, unbeknownst to them, the capacity of the War Rooms to withstand a direct hit was far from sure.

In the seventieth anniversary year of the site becoming operational – a year that coincides with the twenty-fifth anniversary of the Rooms being opened up to the general public – it is timely that the experience of those who worked so assiduously and deprived of daylight should be celebrated with a book that finally gives their story the prominence it deserves.

And there could be no better choice of author than Professor Richard Holmes, one of the most inspired and original biographers of Sir Winston Churchill, and a writer whose works demonstrate an unparalleled understanding of the experience of the common man in war.

Richard's in-depth book charts the discomforts, joys and quirks of daily – and nightly – life in the bunker, as well as giving the wider context of the war that raged above the heads of those living and working there. The history of the Rooms was shaped not only by their almost accidental origins as a 'temporary' solution, but also by the actions of their chief resident and the personalities of those who surrounded him. It is through these stories that Richard outlines a strategic, human and occasionally comic history of this secret site, so important to the success of Britain's war effort.

The Rooms' post-war history has been no less accidental and colourful, and over the years the complex has evolved from a neglected monument to a prize-winning historic site operated by the internationally renowned Imperial War Museum. Decades after the last occupants surfaced into the wrecked streets of Central London, tens of thousands of tourists, schoolchildren and Churchill aficionados yearly spelunk their way down to walk in the footsteps of the great man and his lesser-sung acolytes, receiving an intimate view of the Rooms and the lives of those who lived and worked in them.

Diane Lees
Director-General
Imperial War Museum

1

THE STORY BEHIND THE SECRET

The Second World War was supremely mobile. Armies and navies swirled, in their advances and retreats, over thousands of miles of land and sea, from the icy waters of the North Cape to the deserts of North Africa, and from Pacific atolls to the boundless Russian steppes. In sharp contrast, however, for the leaders of most combatant powers it was a war directed from static headquarters. The last days of Hitler were spent, famously, in his bunker in the heart of Berlin, but as early as 1940 he was forced to take refuge from British bombing in an underground shelter. The bombing of the home islands of Japan forced General Tojo and even the Emperor Hirohito into shelters long before the Japanese surrender. The Allies were very cautious about bombing Rome, where Mussolini had his headquarters in the fifteenth-century Palazzo Venezia, but even so the city was not immune from air attack. Only President Roosevelt and his advisers were wholly safe, for long-range bombers were, as yet, unable to reach Washington.

Britain, within short flying distance of continental Europe, was vulnerable to bombing from the very beginning of the war and all the more so after Germany's conquest of France and Belgium in 1940 brought Luftwaffe bases even closer. This danger had been appreciated before the war and complex plans had been prepared, but never finally decided upon, to protect the nucleus of government and military command from bombing. That this nerve-centre eventually nestled in the basements under the New Public Office (NPO) building off Whitehall was the product of Britain's experience of war, the danger posed by the remorseless rise of air power, and a fair element of chance. The Cabinet War Rooms (CWR) were no purpose-built and cunningly fortified headquarters, but when Winston Churchill visited the underground Cabinet Room, shortly after becoming prime minister in May 1940, he declared: 'This is the room from which I'll direct the war.' A few months later, as the Blitz on London began, the CWR did indeed become central to the direction of the war.

Even as the British governments of the 1930s sought peace, they had, reluctantly, begun to prepare for war. Along with rearming, against the tide of a public opinion powerfully influenced by the experience of 1914–18 and with an undertow of financial gloom, they had to consider what impact a total war waged with modern armaments would have upon great cities, their populations, communications, and the very nervous system of government that made modern war possible.

That the subterranean CWR and the No. 10 Annexe above them were to become the central command point for Britain's conduct of the Second World War was far from predictable. It was an ad hoc answer to the conjuncture of two problems: how best to create an effective high command for a democracy at war, and how to protect it in a conflict in which aerial bombardment was a major threat.

Preparations for war 1902–14

The need for purposeful preparation for major war involving modernisation of the armed forces, coordination of and cooperation between the army and the Royal Navy, and a structure which would combine the primacy of the Cabinet with professional military expertise was recognised early in the twentieth century. The days when British governments had entrusted the conflicts arising from their foreign policy decisions to the commanders of the armies and fleets they had all too often neglected in peacetime were over. The telegraph, telephone and then radio made it easier for governments to intervene in the conduct of military operations, inserting that 'long screwdriver' so resented by modern commanders. War correspondents, using the same communications to file their copy, brought news from the front to a domestic audience in a way that had never been possible before, contributing to political concern about the progress of operations and accelerating politicians' desire to meddle directly in military matters.

The South African War of 1899–1902, when the might of the Empire had been deployed to suppress relatively small numbers of Boer irregulars, had revealed shocking military weaknesses. It also coincided with a general realignment of British foreign policy. France, for so long the traditional adversary, had been badly beaten in the Franco-Prussian War of 1870–71, and the Foreign Office was increasingly inclined to see Imperial Germany, anxious for both colonies and naval might, as the main threat to British power. The Committee of Imperial Defence (CID), an advisory body which was set up in 1902, included senior service officers as well as Cabinet ministers and from 1904 had its own secretariat. It was intended to develop defence policy and coordinate a wide variety of issues by means of specialist sub-committees. Maurice Hankey, then a Royal Marine officer, joined the secretariat in 1908 and became secretary in 1912. A mixture of conscientious civil servant, confidential adviser to prime ministers, and discreet eminence grise, he was, with what one author has called 'a genius for making himself indispensable', a central figure in British defence planning in peace and war in the first half of the twentieth century. First knighted and ultimately raised to the peerage, he was secretary of the War Cabinet during the First World War and then Cabinet secretary from 1919 till 1938. In one sense he was the godfather of the machinery of government described in this book.

The difficulties of directing modern wars, great in themselves, are magnified for parliamentary democracies with market economies. Generals and admirals may indeed be the subject-matter experts, but ultimate control must be retained by prime ministers and their cabinets, while armies and navies in turn depend upon the vigour of the economy and effective utilisation of the nation's manpower. Responsibilities for strategy, the war economy and the allocation of resources cannot easily be separated. Tactical actions can sometimes have disproportionate strategic consequences: conversely, winning battles may bring victory no closer. Just how to establish a system for the effective higher direction of war was a perennial problem for Britain in the first half of the twentieth century.

Although it was theoretically an advisory body, the CID played a crucial role in aligning British military policy with that of France and in underpinning the Anglo-French entente with detailed planning. Military 'conversations' with the French were authorised directly by the foreign secretary, Sir Edward Grey, and the CID meeting in June 1906 considered the dispatch of a British expeditionary force to Belgium or France in the event of a German invasion. At the meeting of 23 August 1911 the Committee accepted the War Office plan for cooperation with the French and ruled against the Admiralty's alternative strategy. It was emphasised that Britain's plan to aid the French in the event of a Franco-German war was not politically binding, and only a handful of ministers knew the extent to which Britain was actually committed to assist France. The role of the CID in this aspect of grand strategy may, however, have been exaggerated. Indeed, it has been suggested that it was not only the Cabinet that was 'sidelined: so too was the CID'.[1] Grey, the service ministers, and senior Foreign and War Office officials were perhaps the only people who fully appreciated the momentous implications of the Anglo-French military discussions.

The *War Book*, which set out the detailed steps to be taken at the outbreak of war and enabled Britain to move rapidly to a war footing in 1914, was the most significant success of the CID. But, with a main committee which rose to over thirty members and a plethora of sub-committees, the CID had tended to withdraw from considering detailed military and naval operational issues after 1908, leaving planning largely in the hands of the General Staff and the Admiralty, who constantly disagreed with each other. Little thought was given to the interrelationship between the economy and the armed forces or to the question of how manpower would be divided between the competing needs of the army, industry and agriculture, although the war effort was ultimately to be as dependent upon manufacture as upon battleships and battalions.

The First World War

Britain's decision-making and command structure during the First World War did not make for either harmonious cooperation between the government and its senior military and naval commanders or a unified direction of the war effort. There were broad problems which were not easily solved. No easy division could be made between the formulation of overall strategy and its practical implementation. The Cabinet was too large a body to conduct a war, and included ministers whose departments had little to do with its prosecution, but, on the other hand, modern conflict demanded the funnelling of all the state's energies into the war effort. The Liberal politician Herbert Asquith, prime minister for the first two years of the war, felt, by and large, that fighting should be left to the experts but that the whole Cabinet was collectively responsible for the war. The breakdown of relations between Winston Churchill, then first lord of the Admiralty, and Admiral Jackie Fisher, the first sea lord; the subsequent animosity between David Lloyd George, who succeeded Asquith as premier, and both Sir Douglas Haig, commander-in-chief of the British Expeditionary Force (BEF), and Sir William Robertson, chief of the Imperial General Staff (CIGS), and the difficulties put in the way of Neville Chamberlain as director of National Service by the War Office are only some of the best-known examples of the tensions between civilians, the 'frocks', and the senior officers, the 'brass hats'.

On the outbreak of war in 1914, the CID was suspended for its duration and was replaced by a succession of bodies, the War Council, the Dardanelles Committee and the War Committee, each utilising the secretariat of the CID. All these committees started with a small number of members dedicated to the direction and coordination of the war, all grew too large, and all encountered the problem of the demarcation between their responsibilities and those of the Cabinet and individual ministers. When Lloyd George became prime minister in December 1916, he combined the functions of the War Committee and the Cabinet by creating a small War Cabinet which took over the old CID secretariat under Maurice Hankey. Theoretically, at least, here was a body able to concentrate solely on the direction and coordination of the war, though in practice it devolved considerable authority to sub-committees, eventually 165 in all, and at the same time had to deal with new ministries conjured up by the war. Historian Peter Simkins has suggested that: 'Lloyd George's War Cabinet tended to operate as a kind of supreme court, arbitrating between the various Government departments and its own inner committees.'[2]

The main problems of prosecuting the First World War were where and how to fight the Central Powers (this debate often focusing on a clash between 'Westerners', who favoured a decision on the Western Front, and 'Easterners', who cast their view more widely), the need to maintain naval supremacy and deal with German submarines, and balancing the demands of an army that put nearly 6 million men through its ranks with the maintenance of the domestic economy and the production of munitions of war. Although an invasion of Britain became progressively less likely after 1914, it could not be ruled out completely, and its threat necessitated the retention of a considerable force within the British isles. Meanwhile, attacks upon civilian and industrial targets by aerial bombardment became a feature of the war. Field Marshal Sir John French's appointment as commander-in-chief Home Forces early in 1916 was a recognition of this new dimension, though French himself was not given a seat on the War Council. It was, though, an index of the fact that political wrangling within the services was scarcely less significant than quarrels between them, that French made no secret of his suspicions of Douglas Haig, who had replaced him in France, and his office in Horse Guards – a short walk from where the War Rooms were to be – became a clearing-house for unhappy senior officers who had come unstuck in

France. In its attempt to solve one problem the government had created another.

Air-raids on Britain during the First World War tend to be little more than footnotes in history, but their psychological impact was considerable. In May 1915 a German airship dropped bombs on London, and from then on attacks continued throughout the war. On 13 June 1917, Gotha bombers mounted a fierce raid on the East End, killing 162 people. During the war, about 300 tons of bombs were dropped on Britain, causing 1,413 deaths. This was an insignificant number in comparison with losses on the Western Front but the sanctity of Britain's 'moat defensive' was broken. French was soon demanding that air squadrons be retained for home defence. Many East Enders took to sheltering in Underground stations on nights when raids seemed likely and some were reluctant to emerge in the morning, behaviour which caused the authorities concern. Limited as they were, these air-raids were intimations of things to come: if this was the effect of limited bombing on morale, what might be the effect of massive air-raids?

No war for ten years

Preparation for war was, not surprisingly, low on the agenda of governments during the twenties and early thirties. Indeed there was a widespread fear that even to contemplate war might somehow bring it closer. Nevertheless, the Committee of Imperial Defence was revived, with the omnipresent Hankey combining the offices of secretary to the Cabinet and the CID. Both Cabinet and CID periodically confirmed the guideline given by the War Cabinet at its last meeting in 1919 that there would not be a war within ten years. A Chiefs of Staffs Committee, a sub-committee of the CID and composed of the heads of the three services (the Royal Air Force had come into being on 1 April 1918) with the prime minister as ex officio chairman, had a responsibility to advise the government on defence and became rather more important than its parent body. By 1936 it had three sub-committees of its own, the Deputy Chiefs of Staff Committee, the Joint Intelligence Committee and the Joint Planning Committee.

What thought was given to future war was dominated by fear of bombing. Despite the 'Ten Year Rule', an Air-Raid Precautions Sub-Committee of the Committee of Imperial Defence was set up in 1924 under Sir John Anderson. It concluded that in a future war 200 tons of bombs would be dropped on London on the first day and that a smaller daily tonnage would be dropped thereafter, resulting in 50,000 casualties within a month. This was not, however, the committee's only concern. Its acceptance that heavy bombing of London would be inevitable led it to consider whether the capital could in fact continue to be the seat of government in wartime.

This was almost to think the unthinkable. During the First World War, the business of government had gone on undisturbed above ground in Whitehall. Any departure of the government from the capital during a war could have a deleterious effect upon national morale and might, some feared, even lead to a panic-stricken exodus of much of the population. Yet London was peculiarly vulnerable. German or French bombers would have to fly over many miles of each other's territory to reach each hostile capital, while London is only a few miles from the coast, with the River Thames pointing to its very heart. Although it recognised the adverse effects on civilian morale of such a move, the committee nevertheless advocated contingency plans for a partial or complete evacuation of Whitehall although, in the event, neither plan was prepared.

The threat of aerial bombardment focused attention on the RAF. Its survival as an independent service rested primarily on the assertion that long-range bombing was to be a major feature of modern warfare. Had the aeroplane been considered simply a means of support to surface forces, acting largely as a supplement to artillery, then air power might have remained a branch of the army and the Royal Navy. In 1918, however, the new independent air force had been carrying out raids into Germany and plans were being made for more extensive missions had the war continued into 1919. Air Chief Marshal Sir Hugh Trenchard, Chief of Air Staff between 1919 and 1929, saw the establishment of an offensive bomber force as essential for the survival of the RAF as an independent service and argued that the next war could be won by the bomber alone. This, and the utility of RAF aircraft in maintaining control of the Middle East by 'Imperial Policing', were powerful arguments in favour of making the RAF the recipient of the lion's share of the money allocated to defence.[3]

Defence policy 1932–39

The 'Ten Year Rule' was eventually abandoned by the Cabinet in March 1932, albeit with the stern warning that 'this must not be taken to justify an expanding expenditure by the Defence Services without regard to the very serious financial and economic situation …'. However, the establishment of a Defence Requirements Committee in 1933 was an early indication of the need for rearmament. Britain faced truly daunting problems. She could not just concern herself with the worsening situation in Europe. A vast empire had to be defended, and with the ending of the Anglo-Japanese Alliance in 1923, relations with her erstwhile ally deteriorated, with a consequent threat to the British position in the Far East. Inevitably, the danger nearest home was given priority and Germany was recognised as the main potential enemy in 1934. Some resources had, however, to be allocated to the Far East.

Britain was a great power which could not afford to go to war. There were sharp limits, both political and economic, to the resources that could be allocated to rearmament. Governments saw little point in defying a neo-pacifist public opinion if this would result in electoral slaughter – in late 1933, the deputy leader of the Labour Party, Clement Attlee, declared his party 'unalterably opposed to anything in the nature of rearmament' – while too rapid a rearmament programme was likely to produce a balance of payments deficit.

Colonel Hastings ('Pug') Ismay became deputy secretary to the CID in 1936 and the secretariat was further strengthened by the appointment of Major Leslie Hollis, a Royal Marine, as assistant secretary:

Hollis soon became secretary to the increasingly important Joint Planning Committee. Ismay described the spring of 1936 as a turning point in defence policy, the time when faith in a new international order as the defender of security was fatally weakened and it was realised that preparations had to be made for national defence.[4]

In February that year the new post of minister for coordination of defence was created prior to the announcement, in the Defence White Paper of March, of a substantially enhanced rearmament programme. The minister was to be responsible for supervising the CID, and had authority to convene and chair meetings of the Chiefs of Staff. The new ministry had been vigorously demanded by Churchill, who hoped to head it himself, but Hankey demurred, feeling that the existing government machine was quite capable of implementing the new programme. The quip that the appointment of Sir Thomas Inskip to the post was 'the most cynical thing that has been done since Caligula appointed his horse a Consul' is often attributed to the disappointed Churchill, but seems to have come from his close friend Professor Frederick Lindemann, who may, however, have been repeating a Churchillian bon mot. Inskip had no experience of defence and it is probable that his appointment was an assurance both to Hankey and to the head of the Treasury, Sir Warren Fisher, that the new minister would not 'rock the Whitehall boat'.[5] In his memoirs Hollis describes Inskip's appointment as 'inauspicious'[6] and Ismay, generously feeling it unfair to blame Inskip, thought he had 'failed to make any significant contribution to our war-making capacity'.[7] An alternative view is that:

> Despite the jibes of his opponents, Inskip proved to be an effective chairman of the Chiefs of Staff Committee; 'his lawyer's mind saw clearly to the heart of the problem and ... he expressed his views with admirable clarity and unusual brevity.' Chamberlain did not believe that it was necessary for the Minister of Co-ordination to be a strategist, it was enough that he should ensure that 'strategical problems are fairly and thoroughly worked out by strategists'; in other words, he was a man to prick the bubble of the inflated demands which all service chiefs make as part of their job.[8]

Inskip was a minister without a ministry and had little executive authority: his job was coordination. Though his policy of rearmament within the limits of the economic stability that Chamberlain saw as the 'fourth arm of defence' is easy to criticise, he was certainly working within the broad remit of government policy.

In the autumn of 1936, the issue of a War Cabinet and its relations with military advisers was reviewed. This Cabinet was to be like that of the latter years of the First World War and would receive professional advice on military affairs from the Chiefs of Staff, the Deputy Chiefs and the Joint Planning and Intelligence Committees. Provision was made for possible disagreements between the Cabinet and the military, with the chiefs having to record their dissent if their advice was overruled. That November it was argued by the director of Military Operations and the director of Intelligence that all key military staff should work in the same building as the War Cabinet.

The Conservative politician Neville Chamberlain, first as chancellor (1931–37) and then as prime minister (1937–40), was the major influence on British defence policy in the 1930s. His priorities in the allocation of resources were the RAF and then the Royal Navy: he regarded the army as 'an insurance if deterrence failed, rather than the primary deterrent in itself' and, in common, it must be said, with the majority of professional soldiers, he was notably lukewarm about the creation of an expeditionary force to help defend the Low Countries and France, a view he was not to change until January 1939.[9]

Fears of air-raids had grown apace. The prevailing wisdom of politicians and defence experts in the 1930s was that, in the words of Stanley Baldwin (three times premier, latterly in 1935–7), 'the bomber would always get through' and would cause untold damage and a massive death toll. By 1936, the Air Ministry calculated that casualties would be around 200,000 a week, with some 60,000 killed. As well as reluctantly rearming, the government had to look once more at the need for what was known, in the jargon of the day, as Air Raid Precautions (ARP).

One apparent answer to the threat of destruction from the air was to match the bombing capacity of a potential opponent in order to deter him: some have seen this reliance on deterrence as a forerunner of the policy of mutually assured destruction adopted during the Cold War. As the Conservative politician Harold Macmillan was to put it: 'We thought of air warfare in 1938 rather as people think of nuclear warfare today.'[10]

This belief led not only to the RAF being put at

the forefront of British rearmament after 1934, but to the main emphasis being placed upon the supply of bombers, on the assumption that bombing would be the decisive strategy in a future war, a policy enthusiastically embraced by Chamberlain at the Treasury. It was only in 1937, after Inskip acknowledged that Britain could not afford to keep up in the race for bombers, that priority was switched to defence and to Fighter Command. The new emphasis was on increasing the novel technology of defence (radar, anti-aircraft guns and searchlights) and on setting up production lines for a new generation of fighter aircraft, a policy that would lead to Britain in 1940 being able to outpace Germany in the manufacture of modern fighters.

As the government reluctantly increased defence spending, reviewed the readiness and efficiency of the armed forces and looked once more at proposals for Air Raid Precautions, the questions of the national command structure and the threat posed to it by bombing became intimately related. The structure of the high command was crucial. The necessity for interservice cooperation in preparations for war could hardly be denied, especially as war might begin suddenly, with an immediate air attack upon Britain. The services, characteristically, had conflicting priorities. The Air Ministry was an advocate of a unified command, but the Admiralty and War Office sought to protect their independence. The recognition, not only in the mind of the public but also to a large extent in government circles, of the crucial importance of air power persuaded admirals and generals that the needs of the Royal Navy and the army would be subordinated to those of the RAF within any unified command. The Air Ministry, in contrast, was confident that its needs would be seen as paramount, and was convinced that the speed of air operations necessitated equally rapid decisions. It saw, therefore, major advantages in a unified command structure. Arguing that the existing system of formal consultations between staffs was inadequate, it proposed in 1937 'that all land and sea and air operations should be controlled by a Committee of Supreme Commanders, a "Generalissimo in commission" superior to commanders-in-chief in specific theatres of war and working directly under the Chiefs of Staff'.[11] The Air Staff also favoured the creation of a Joint Operations and Intelligence Staff.

These proposals were rejected by the Deputy Chiefs of Staff (DCOS), who continued to believe that cooperation and 'lateral correlation' rather than unified command were sufficient. However, confusion during combined air defence exercises persuaded the DCOS that further moves towards closer cooperation were necessary. In December 1937, they agreed that a 'Central Authority' should be set up and should consist of the 'COS, DCOS, Joint Planning Staff and probably an Air-Raid Precautions Staff as well, and it should be housed in a "Central War Room"'.[12]

The idea of a Central War Room was accepted, and suggestions were made as to a location – either the Chief of the Imperial General Staff's (CIGS's) offices in Whitehall Gardens, or in Richmond Terrace – but the DCOS committee, despite its keenness for cooperation, was resolutely opposed to the war room's having a combined staff. The Admiralty was even more hostile than the War Office to anything that went beyond simple collaboration. What had emerged by the summer of 1938 was the concept of a Central War Room in which the single-service Chiefs of Staff would meet and confer, informed of up-to-date intelligence supplied and correlated by all three services. This War Room would not be an operational headquarters. The chiefs and their deputies would debate there and make decisions, but those policies would be implemented by individual service staffs.

The supreme control of war would remain in the government's hands, although it would be advised by the chiefs and their deputies. As the Cabinet was too large, it was envisaged in 1938 that, in the initial stages of the war, control should be exercised by a sub-committee of the Cabinet, which would swiftly be superseded by a War Cabinet along First World War lines. As civilian and military elements would need to be in close proximity to each other, it was decided that the War Cabinet should be in the same building as the chiefs' war room. Hankey proposed that a 'National HQ' should be built to house the War Cabinet, chiefs and staffs, with wings to accommodate central staffs of the services, the ARP Department and the Foreign Office. The CID developed this proposal in 1938 and plans were made for an 'Emergency War HQ', but war came before such a building was even begun. In August 1939 it was intended that the government would form a War Cabinet immediately war broke out and to this end the Cabinet and CID secretariats were merged. As soon as war was declared a Ministerial Committee for War Coordination was set up as a Cabinet sub-committee to exercise day-to-day control of the conduct of the war. Plans for the effective prosecution of a war thus pointed towards a small War Cabinet in close touch with the senior echelons of the three forces, each of which should be in lateral contact with the others.

Protecting the High Command

The downside of a small, unified command was that a single air-raid could wipe it out, instantly destroying the essential central organs of military and civil control. A devastating attack was expected as soon as war broke out, and it might be accurately targeted, for spies could surely discover the location of the new headquarters: indeed, even the building activity intended to protect it might actually betray it. No alternative solutions were perfect. Dispersal did away with many of the advantages of unified control from a single site. A shadow system of duplicating the system of command apparatus was a possibility but had obvious disadvantages.

As 1940 was to show, pre-war assessments had vastly overestimated the damage and casualties that bombing by the Luftwaffe was likely to cause. Immediately prior to the war emphasis was placed on the risk of surprise attack, either immediately after a declaration of war or even without one. By early 1940, estimates of casualties had been scaled down to 16,000 a day and, in fact, there were 147,000 fatal or serious casualties during the whole of the war, 80,000 of them in London.[13] This was bad enough, but was not on the scale that had been feared. The scope and effectiveness of German strategic air power were also exaggerated. Germany was indeed building the most powerful air force in the world, but it was primarily a tactical instrument designed to support an army: heavy, long-range bombers were not being produced. Yet, if the immediate threat was exaggerated, the fears were understandable and the later years of the Second World War would indeed demonstrate that raids by heavy bombers could bring about the worst nightmares of the thirties.

Convinced of the destruction that bombing would bring, the government was nevertheless torn between the need to make preparations for civil defence and fear that by doing so it would inspire panic among the population. 'For years, the government kept secret that it was even considering civil defence, for fear that the very mention of air raids precautions (ARP) would cause the public panic that it was believed would ensue from air-raids', writes Malcolm Smith. 'The Air Raid Precautions Bill was not introduced into Parliament until November 1937, and was then rushed into law by January 1938.'[14] As the European situation deteriorated, fear of bombing accelerated preparations for a war that most still hoped would never happen: plans were developed for the evacuation of children, air-raid precautions including the building of shelters, and the stockpiling of thousands of cardboard coffins in stores around London. The Home Office was concerned that communications between central government and the provinces might be cut by enemy action and, just before the Munich crisis of 1938, it established thirteen regional commissioners whose job it was to take over the reins of government should this happen. Relations between these commissioners and ARP officers appointed by local authorities were strained during the Munich crisis, not least because the government chose to keep the appointment of the commissioners secret.[15] Even these defensive arrangements were not safe from influential neo-pacifist opinion, which argued that they brought war closer because they allowed people to imagine that it might be survivable, and a number of left-wing local authorities refused to cooperate for this very reason.[16] The financing of civil defence was yet another problem. Urban local authorities complained that protecting their populations would cost much more than the protection of rural populations, yet the grants available did not allow for a distinction.

The question raised by Sir John Anderson's committee a decade earlier, as to whether devastating bombing raids would make the operation of government in the centre of London impossible, was considered with a new urgency. A small War Cabinet housed in close proximity to the Chiefs of Staff would indeed be an inviting target for enemy bombers. There was vacillation over conflicting plans for ensuring the survival of the high command. The options were broadly threefold. First, leave the headquarters in Whitehall but shield it in a bomb-proof shelter; second, evacuate it and key government departments to the capital's suburbs; or third – the so-called 'Black Move' – leave London altogether and put the centre of government and military command in the West Country.

The Warren Fisher Committee in 1936 and the Rae Committee in 1937 both considered the problem. They agreed that evacuation and dispersal from central London were the answer, but did not envisage that there would be much time: bombers might arrive within six hours of a declaration of war. In the event, there was compromise, with dispersal and remaining in hardened accommodation in Whitehall being planned alternatives.

The Rae Committee thought that it would be necessary to remove the government from central London to areas less vulnerable to bombers based on continental airfields, though it was not foreseen at this time that airfields close to the Channel would be available to the Luftwaffe. Its report recommended a division of officials into Groups A and B, those who were 'essential' to the prosecution of the war and those not directly concerned with operations. Ministers, the central command and all Group A staff could be moved to the suburbs of north-west London but, if buildings there were not deemed safe enough, a further move to the West Country would be necessary. Once Group A staff had left Whitehall, Group B staff would proceed directly to the Midlands and the north-west. It was also recommended that arrangements should be made for the evacuation of the Royal Family as well as Parliament, the BBC, the Bank of England and other crucial institutions and national treasures. In the event, the Royal Family scorned evacuation, but the National Gallery collection spent the war in a quarry in North Wales and the Bank of England not only moved to the Hampshire village of Overton but shifted over 2,000 tons of its gold to Canada. The BBC's variety production went to Bristol and senior staff to a stately home near Evesham, while the Post Office's senior managers decamped to Harrogate.

It is easy, with hindsight, to see the various plans

as half-hearted or tentative preparations beset with contradictions. The planners were, however, working to an unknown timetable for a war that might still be avoided. That no firm decision was taken as to which option to select meant, though, that none was pursued with single-minded consistency. Only in May 1938 did Ismay, aware that elaborate solutions would take time, which seemed to him to be in short supply, order the Office of Works to survey Whitehall and find the safest place for an emergency centre. It was, at first, envisaged that this emergency War Room would be for the use of the Chiefs of Staff, the Deputy Chiefs of Staff, the Joint Planning Committee and the Joint Intelligence Committee. It was not to be an operations centre, and decisions by the Chiefs of Staff would be implemented by the war rooms of the individual services. Not until May 1939 was it decided that the Cabinet should also be housed in the Central War Room.

The Central War Rooms take shape

The Office of Works concluded that the most suitable facilities in Whitehall were in the basement of the New Public Offices, at the corner of Great George Street and Storey's Gate, which had a steel-framed structure. The CID concurred that these rooms were suitable, Ismay was put in charge of the project, and work began on their conversion. These rooms, at the very centre of this book's story, were destined to become the focus of national command in the Second World War, but their conversion and reinforcement were not seen at the time as anything but temporary and emergency measures, a stop-gap until either a purpose-built headquarters in central London was constructed, citadels in the suburbs were ready or a wholesale evacuation from the capital had been properly planned. It was only in 1939 that the policy of staying in Whitehall for as long as possible even without deep shelters gained favour. At the end of 1938, the Office of Works was ordered to provide all Whitehall departments with protected rooms large enough to enable a nucleus staff of 100 to 150 to operate during air-raids; in addition to the Cabinet War Rooms there were to be hardened War Rooms for the service headquarters and for the ARP, protected by concrete slabs and sandbags, gas-proofed and able to sustain the collapse of the buildings above them.

A move to citadels in the suburbs by Cabinet and key defence departments had the advantage of retaining government in London, albeit not in crowded Whitehall but in scattered nodes which bombers would have difficulty in locating. But there was also a fear that the effects of bombing might lead to civil disorder and the breakdown of London's infrastructure. Would the suburbs really be much safer, and would the activity of fortifying suburban strongholds alert the enemy to their existence?

Nevertheless there were weighty arguments in favour of evacuation and dispersal. The Air Ministry was profoundly pessimistic about the possibility of Cabinet, Chiefs of Staff and service ministries being able to continue to exercise control in a city it expected to be devastated. Even if they remained safe in their underground bunkers, they could be cut off from the rest of the country. On the other hand evacuation would be an enormous task. Prior to war it would have to be done with discretion in order not to alert an enemy and perhaps impel a pre-emptive attack, and so as not to demoralise the population. If evacuation and dispersal were left till conflict seemed imminent, the very action might accelerate the slide of crisis into a war. As the Rae scheme of evacuation would take at least seven days notice to execute, its implementation at the very beginning of a war would cause confusion and damage efficiency at a crucial time.

A variation on the Rae plan, recommended by an interdepartmental conference, was the 'Insurance' plan by which each essential department should set up a 'Nucleus Operations Staff'. These shadow staffs would, when war appeared imminent, leave London for safer places: the Naval nucleus for Rosyth and the army, RAF and ARP for Bentley Priory, the headquarters of the RAF's Fighter Command near Harrow. From these safer havens they could control operations in the event of their parent departments being destroyed. During the Munich Crisis a version of this plan was tested when the Navy and RAF sent operational staff to destinations outside London. It was not a success. There was confusion, with officials from different departments almost coming 'to blows in their attempts to claim one of the [Oxford] colleges'.[17] The activity compromised security, and it was discovered that the plan clashed with arrangements for civilian evacuation. The Rae plan was, therefore, modified again in October 1938. Group A Staff would stay in London for at least ten days and Group B would move first. Insurance staffs would move to protected accommodation in north-west London and preparations in the West Country should be accelerated.

The Office of Works was understandably confused and irritated. Plans kept changing, and it had to locate and bomb-proof accommodation in the suburbs and also find buildings for a government and service staffs in the countryside, while proposals for either new fortified buildings or underground shelters in Whitehall were still being mooted. The basement of the General Post Office's research centre in Dollis Hill was earmarked for the Emergency War Headquarters; it was to become a 'citadel' to house the Cabinet and the Chiefs of Staff. It was to replicate the layout of the suite of rooms under the New Public Offices. Protected by a massive slab of concrete, it was expected to be ready early in 1940. In August 1939, the CID was told that the Admiralty and Air Ministry War Rooms at Cricklewood and Harrow would soon be completed.

The Office of Works had always preferred the idea of evacuation and made it clear that being forced to work on the north-west suburbs scheme had prevented it from setting up suitable war rooms in the West Country. Early in 1939, the Cabinet took its advice and agreed that if bombed out of Whitehall, Group A Staff would go directly to the west but insisted that preparations in the suburbs would still go ahead. It was expected in July that there would, by the end of the year, be four basements in the suburbs capable of withstanding direct hits by a 500 lb bomb. The Naval and RAF suburban war rooms were due to be finished by autumn and the Cabinet citadel at Dollis Hill was also nearing completion.

The search for suitable locations in the West Country and Midlands also went ahead and in January 1939 the CID authorised preparations in Worcester, Gloucester, Malvern, Cheltenham and Evesham. These plans added a new layer of complexity, for there was now a long-term and a short-term scheme. In the long term, the Cabinet would go to Cheltenham, the War Office to Tewkesbury and the Air Ministry and Home Security to Gloucester. In the short term, it was eventually agreed that the Cabinet would be based at Hindlip Hall, on the road from Worcester to Droitwich, while the Admiralty went to Malvern, the Air Ministry to Hartlebury and the War Office to Droitwich. The House of Commons was to go to Stratford on Avon.

Had war come a year or so later than it did, then there could have been a host of options open to the government with a number of fortified headquarters in the north-west suburbs and prepared facilities in the west. As it was, preparations in the suburbs were fairly advanced and were expected to be complete in 1940, and there were contingency plans for the 'Black Move', with Spetchley Manor, close to Hindlip Hall, earmarked for the prime minister and immediate staff, and other houses allocated to the secretariat and other ministers.

The least thought had actually been given to the option which turned out to be the one chosen in September 1939: staying put in Whitehall. Relatively little preparation had been made, apart from the work on the Central War Room under the NPO and provision of other protected basement offices in Whitehall. Those grand plans for a protected Whitehall, mooted as early as 1933, when the provision of bomb-proof accommodation for the Cabinet had first been raised, had come to naught. A putative purpose-built Emergency War Headquarters in Whitehall Gardens, with a protected basement with working space for 1,000 officials and offices for the War Cabinet, had been opposed on grounds of cost and the psychological damage its very existence might do to morale. Another proposal had been for a Deep Tunnel System which would have involved burying steel tubes, like those used by London Underground, in which working space for 700 personnel would be provided. After the recommendation of evacuation by the Warren Fisher and Rae Committees, these plans were put aside.

Despite Chamberlain's assertion that the Munich agreement of 1938 meant 'peace for our time', plans for fortifying Whitehall were revived. The CID was by this time in favour of the projected War Cabinet staying in central London for as long as possible while, in any case, the citadels in the suburbs were not due for completion until 1940 at the earliest. A variety of plans for tunnels and protected basements was mooted, but few practical steps had been taken by the time that war broke out.

Meanwhile, work had continued, in the basement of the NPO building, on what were to become the CWR. Ismay had been given responsibility by the Chiefs of Staff for supervising their preparation but delegated the task to Hollis, who was in turn assisted by Eric de Normann of the Office of Works and Lawrence Burgis from the Cabinet Office. The rooms were ten feet below ground level along a central corridor and were used for storing archives: work began on emptying them in

June 1938. By the end of that month a number of rooms had been cleared. Rooms 61A–65A were allocated, 65A for use by the Cabinet and 64 for the Chiefs of Staff while the larger room between them, 65, was to be the Map Room. An immense amount of work had to be done. Communications were installed, with batteries of colour-coded telephones, rooms had to be soundproofed and given greater protection, and plans were made for gas-proofing the entire complex. More rooms were required, and the warren expanded into Rooms 60, 60A and 61. The BBC supplied two sets of broadcast equipment, and connections were made with its studios in Maida Vale and Broadcasting House. The Munich Crisis accelerated activity and a mechanical ventilation system was installed, while the imminent prospect of many people working underground for long periods led Hollis to demand better facilities.[18] In December 1938, the roof was reinforced with steel girders, but the War Rooms were never fully bombproof and extra protection was continually added as the war progressed.

While Leslie Hollis's importance can scarcely be overstated, his account of the preparation of the War Rooms is somewhat misleading. He suggests that there was a definite plan 'to create a war headquarters which would give the greatest possible protection against bombing, and from which the country could be governed and the war directed even under air attack' and that, from the beginning, it was accepted that 'the accommodation provided was to include air conditioning, secure communications, an independent water and lighting supply, hospital arrangements, and sleeping quarters.'[19] In fact, the War Rooms evolved as the international situation deteriorated and revised estimates were made of the numbers of staff that were likely to be based there. The Office of Works regarded the arrangements as purely temporary and was reluctant to authorise expenditure or to provide more space in the NPO, while 'The question of domestic accommodation became a bone of contention between the Office of Works and the CID Secretariat early in 1939'.[20] That the War Rooms were able to function from seven days before war broke out owed much to the determination of Hollis, Burgis and de Normann and the support they received from Ismay, rather than the foresight of planners or the consistency of their work. From that point of view the rooms were, perhaps, definitively British.

All this activity was likely to attract attention, and raised the question of security. It was decided that service personnel rather than civilian cleaners should do the cleaning, and a detachment of Royal Marines under the command of Captain Adams was detailed to provide guards and orderlies. But what about the noise and the disruption, which were impossible to keep secret? Here the involvement of George Rance, an Office of Works official, was a master-stroke. He was a long-standing figure about Whitehall, responsible for ordering furniture for various government departments, and under his aegis the clearing and furnishing of rooms could be made to seem routine: after all, he did it all the time. All equipment, including maps, intended for the Central War Room was simply addressed to Mr Rance.

The Cabinet War Rooms have been thought of as a well-kept secret but their preparation was not unobserved. Their conversion and reinforcement disrupted the work of departments and was both visible and audible:

> Alexander Cadogan, Permanent [Under] Secretary at the Foreign Office, complained that he was constantly having to shift personnel to and fro to allow access to the new 'War Room' being constructed in the basement; in early January [1939] the *Evening Standard* reported 'furious drilling and clanging' in King Charles Street and beneath the quadrangles of the Treasury and Foreign Office.[21]

A further reason for the government wishing the preparations to be discreet was the worry about the effects of any shelters for ministers and officials on civilian attitudes to the government. There had long been concern that bombing would result in disorder and anger that might be directed against the authorities. The protection of the higher organs of the state and of command was essential, but preparations might easily be construed as those in power looking after themselves while not doing enough for the population as a whole, especially the thousands who did not have gardens and so could not benefit from the new shelters, designed in 1938 and named after Sir John Anderson, minister responsible for Air Raid Precautions, which had to be dug in.

By the outbreak of war in September 1939, in the words of Nigel de Lee:

> ... despite the feverish activity of the previous year, the only facilities actually ready for use were those

> temporary emergency suites which had been prepared in haste in late spring 1938, and expanded in the teeth of opposition and difficulty in spring 1939. The most effective of these improvised arrangements was the Cabinet War Room, which functioned continuously until the surrender of Japan. [22]

Whether, after years of vacillation, the government's late decision to stay in Whitehall, in a most imperfectly fortified CWR, against the advice of the Air Ministry, was sensible was yet to be seen. Britain went to war in September 1939 with her national headquarters reflecting more than a dash of that amateurishness sometimes held to characterise her approach to war.

The novelist Dennis Wheatley, who worked in the Cabinet War Rooms from December 1941, commented:

> Hitler never envisaged being driven into a cellar; so when at last the blasting of Berlin by the Russian guns forced him and his personal staff to seek refuge in the Reich Chancellery they had to descend into a maze of chilly, hastily furnished concrete rooms having none of the amenities of a Great Headquarters. In Britain, on the other hand, the Committee of Imperial Defence had had the forethought to take precautions against the annihilation of its 'brain' by heavy bombing.[23]

He was, as we have seen, being more than a little generous: but then, he was an author who travelled to the wilder shores of fiction.

2

THE BLAST OF WAR

It was one of the most poignant broadcasts in history. On Sunday 3 September 1939, families all over Britain gathered round their wireless sets at 11.15 a.m. and listened grimly while the prime minister, Neville Chamberlain, announced, in a flat, almost toneless voice, that the country was at war with Germany. A massive and immediate air attack was the almost universal expectation, and in London warning sirens sounded soon after the prime minister had finished speaking. A civilian in the suburbs remembered it well:

> Surely not, they can't be coming already, and with uncertainty and not quite sure what action to take, we all went to the window. The siren had stopped and the road outside was deserted apart for two middle-aged gentlemen who were running like the wind.[1]

In Whitehall it was not much different. Hastings Ismay reached his office in Richmond Terrace and found that his staff had faithfully observed instructions:

> ... for the first and probably the last time; and there was nothing for it but to follow them to the shelter in the basement. It was very crowded and one or two of the girls were in tears. A year later they were to be seen stepping out into the fiercest blitz without a qualm.[2]

John Colville, then a third secretary in the diplomatic service, had been assigned to the new Ministry of Economic Warfare. He was sitting in its temporary headquarters in the London School of Economics when the sirens wailed:

> It was widely believed that London would be reduced to rubble within minutes of war being declared, as recently depicted to an alarmed populace in the film of H. G. Wells' book called *The Shape of Things to Come*; and it seemed as if this was indeed about to happen. So we scuttled, preserving what semblance of nonchalance we could, to the air-raid shelter.[3]

It had been a false alarm.

Ismay and his staff had, however, been busy and the plans to put the country on a war footing had been implemented. Ismay was by now secretary of the Committee of Imperial Defence (CID), having succeeded an officer who had held the post briefly, after Hankey's retirement in 1938. He took over just one of Hankey's roles, for it had been recognised that Hankey's burden was an almost intolerable one, and that Sir Edward Bridges, a brilliant career civil servant who, like so many of his generation, had served with distinction in the First World War, would become secretary to the Cabinet. Inskip had been replaced as minister for the coordination of defence by Lord Chatfield, a former first sea lord, in the same year, and so 1938 had seen a considerable turnover of key personnel. Hankey had, however, bequeathed a durable legacy for Ismay: Leslie Hollis and Ian Jacob (a field marshal's son commissioned into the Royal Engineers in 1918) had all been identified by him.

From the spring of 1939, war had seemed increasingly probable, and the CID was kept busy. The *War Book* was carefully checked and Britain could have been put on a war footing earlier if it had not still been hoped that war might yet be avoided and that taking further steps to prepare for it might make it more likely. As Ismay has written: 'The dispatch of a single telegram of three words, "Institute Precautionary Stage", would have set in motion innumerable measures of infinite variety all over the world.' Nevertheless, during August the heads of government departments met daily and agreed on those precautionary moves which could not be postponed and these were then authorised by the Cabinet. By 31 August the precautionary stage had been almost completed incrementally.[4]

The Central War Rooms, as they were then formally known, were opened up on 27 August and were visited by the King on 30 August. On 3 September, the day war was declared, the chiefs of staff were already in conference in the building and, when Ismay interrupted their meeting to tell them that the country was at war, they received the news without comment. William Dickson, an RAF officer who later rose to the rank of air vice-marshal, was on duty in the Map Room when the sirens began; plots of enemy planes were already being marked up. A telephone rang and the prime minister's secretary enquired whether it was safe for Chamberlain to leave No. 10 to go the Commons. Dickson went to the chiefs of staff to report this and '[Air Chief Marshal Sir Cyril] Newall got on the telephone to Dowding [CinC Fighter Command].' The false alarm had in fact been given immediately the radar was switched on, because of 'bluebottles or something' in the works.[5]

In many respects, Britain had learned from the experience of an earlier war. A War Cabinet on the Lloyd George model was set up. The CID was dissolved and its secretariat and that of the Cabinet merged into a single body under Sir Edward Bridges, though it had two sub-sections. One dealt with civil matters and was headed by Bridges himself with Sir Rupert Howarth as his deputy and Lawrence Burgis as his assistant; the other dealt with military affairs and was headed by Ismay with Hollis as his senior assistant. Each section had eight or more assistant secretaries. The 'hard core' of the military assistant secretaries at the beginning of the war consisted, according to Ismay, of Captain Angus Mitchell RN, Wing Commander William Elliot, Major Ian Jacob, Captain Cornwall-Jones and Lieutenant Coleridge RN.[6]

Chamberlain's first intention was to have a small War Cabinet of about six ministers, but, rather like Lloyd George's War Cabinet, it grew. Hankey, now a peer, who became a minister without portfolio and a member of the War Cabinet, had argued that it should be composed of senior ministers unencumbered by departmental responsibilities. Having decided that Winston Churchill, a leading critic of his appeasement policy, should, now that war had come, be given office, Chamberlain first thought of bringing him into the War Cabinet as a minister without a department. But the prospect of Churchill being left 'to roam over the whole field of policy' as David Margesson, the government's chief whip, acutely put it, was so daunting that it was decided that he should go to the Admiralty (in the very post he had held at the beginning of the First World War) but have a seat in the War Cabinet. This necessitated bringing in the other service ministers, Leslie Hore-Belisha (secretary of state for war) and Kingsley Wood (secretary of state for air), who were already complaining that, if they were not in the body controlling the war, their positions would be weakened.[7] Thus, even before its first meeting on 3 September 1939, the War Cabinet had grown to nine. There were the prime minister and three ministers without departments, Sir Samuel Hoare (lord privy seal), Lord Chatfield (minister for defence coordination) and Lord Hankey. It was impossible to exclude Sir John Simon (chancellor of the exchequer) and Lord Halifax (foreign secretary), and then, of course, there were the three service ministers.

The Chiefs of Staff Committee promised far better coordination between the armed services than had existed during the First World War. At the beginning of the war, the chiefs were the first sea lord, Admiral Sir Dudley Pound, the chief of the Imperial General Staff, General Sir Edmund Ironside, and the chief of the Air Staff, Air Chief Marshal Sir Cyril Newall. The chiefs of staff reported directly to the War Cabinet but this had the disadvantage of involving the Cabinet in the formulation of military policy at an early stage, with the risk of its becoming swamped with excessive detail. An answer was found in the setting up of an intermediary body, the Standing Ministerial Committee of Military Coordination, with Lord Chatfield as chairman, but this brought with it the disadvantages of duplicating discussion and sometimes contradicting the conclusions of the Chiefs of Staff. There were essentially two problems, neither entirely soluble, of relations between the services, each of which had its own priorities, and those between the military and the government.

Arrangements had also been made for a Supreme War Council, consisting of the heads of the British and French governments and their senior advisers, which would facilitate Anglo-French cooperation, and its first meeting took place shortly after the beginning of the war. Its decision that, in the event of a German invasion of Belgium, the Allied forces would move into Belgium so as to hold the Germans as far east as possible was to have far-reaching consequences. The danger of thus leaving prepared defences to engage in a mobile war against an enemy who might be better prepared was appreciated by Lieutenant-General Alan Brooke, then commanding a corps in the British Expeditionary Force (BEF), and later to become an outstanding chief of the Imperial General Staff, later ennobled as Viscount Alanbrooke.[8]

The Bore War

After all the frenzied preparations, the BEF and the French army had little engagement with the Germans during the first eight months of a conflict called the *drôle de guerre* by the French and the 'bore war' by the British. The real fighting took place in central Europe. Britain had ostensibly gone to war over the integrity of Poland, but Poland was quickly overrun by the Germans from the west and then by the Soviet Union from the east, the two invaders dividing the spoils between them. There was no help from Britain or France. The French army, after a token advance, retreated to what it imagined was the security of the 'great carapace' of the Maginot Line, and thereafter both it and the BEF remained on French territory, unable even to move forward into the punctiliously neutral Belgium. The RAF bombed German warships in Brunsbüttel and Wilhelmshaven harbours but, as only military targets were to be attacked and civilian casualties avoided, had to content itself with dropping leaflets over Germany. There were some German air attacks on Scapa Flow, and a German plane ventured up the Thames estuary in November but turned back after encountering anti-aircraft fire. The only bombs came from the Irish Republican Army whose campaign for a united Ireland was unaffected by the outbreak of a rather wider war.

However, one service was involved in serious combat. The Royal Navy lost the aircraft carrier HMS *Courageous* to one U-boat in the Western Approaches and the battleship HMS *Royal Oak* to another which boldly penetrated the anchorage at Scapa Flow, but had a considerable victory when the pocket battleship

Graf Spee was scuttled in the estuary of the River Plate rather than face the British cruisers which were waiting for her. The sinking of the *Graf Spee* boosted the popularity of Winston Churchill as first lord of the Admiralty, as did the interception, controversially in Norwegian territorial waters, of the *Altmark*, a German supply ship carrying British prisoners.

What was to become known as the 'Home Front' remained quiet. Children were evacuated from the capital but then many returned, everyone assiduously carried a gas-mask for a few weeks and then tended to leave it at home. Cinemas and theatres closed but then reopened. Reservists and conscripts were called up, regiments embarked, and a blackout was enforced, leading to a marked increase in traffic accidents, but life returned to a semblance of normality. This, the period from September 1939 to May 1940, was, we are told, the time of the 'Phoney War' but, as the adjective suggests, the term was thought up by American journalists. Ismay in his *Memoirs* uses the rather more elegant alternative the 'Twilight War', though this is evidently retrospective. 'There is no real war', wrote socialite, politician and diarist 'Chips' Channon. 'Hitler is indeed shrewd. Is he trying to bore us into peace?'[9] Chamberlain was fond of saying that it was 'better to be bored than bombed' but the combination of all the inconveniences of war without much action made for an atmosphere of discontent and cynicism.

In Whitehall, as elsewhere, normality seemed to have surfaced once again. Cabinet ministers and senior civil servants followed their usual daily routine, lunched at their clubs and left London at weekends, though the prime minister decreed that three ministers must remain in London. Chamberlain and his wife were able to walk around St James's Park with only a single detective following at a discreet distance and he spent two out of every three weekends at Chequers, rarely taking a private secretary with him.[10] Ilene Adams, then an eighteen-year-old secretary, was working in the secretariat in Richmond Terrace and remembered Chamberlain as a real gentleman who always spoke to her and, despite the war, would doff his hat if they met in the park.[11]

Once war had begun, the government had yet again to decide whether or not to stay in London, for just because there had not yet been air-raids did not mean they would not come soon. On 6 September, the Chiefs of Staff recommended that all non-essential staff should be sent away from London and the Cabinet ordered preliminary measures for the evacuation of all government staff but went no further for fear of undermining civilian morale. A 'Slow Yellow' move was, however, put into operation and Group B personnel (those not directly concerned with operations) of the Admiralty and Air Ministry went to Bath and Harrogate respectively while the War Office Mapping Section went to Cheltenham.

Contingency planning for a 'Black Move' to the west continued. The shift to various houses in Worcestershire would take place in two phases: in the first the War Cabinet and senior staff would go to Hindlip Hall and the prime minister and his personal staff to Spetchley Manor; and in the second phase the prime minister and Sir Horace Wilson, permanent secretary to the treasury, would move into Hindlip Hall, leaving their secretariat at Spetchley, while the Cabinet secretariat would go to Bevere House and other members of the War Cabinet would be accommodated at other country houses in the area. The space available at Hindley Hall was increased by building huts, soon camouflaged, in the grounds. By early October 1939 the Hall was ready for occupation. The 'Black Move' never took place but the arrangements were justified as, from June 1940, it was not just bombing that had to be feared but invasion too.

While Chamberlain was prime minister, the Cabinet met in the underground War Rooms on only one occasion, in October 1939. In the absence of air-raids there really was not much point in using a cramped underground quarters when 10 Downing Street was available. The main part of the defence staff remained in Richmond Terrace, having moved there from Whitehall Gardens just before the war began. The Chiefs of Staff, however, met at least daily and sometimes two or three times a day, usually in the War Rooms but often elsewhere. The Joint Planning Committee (JPC) and its staff were regular users of the War Rooms and their rapid expansion had, by 1940, led to overcrowding in the basement. The Map Room was manned around the clock from just before the outbreak of war by nine plotters assisted by two clerks, supervised by senior members of the JPC. Information came to the Map Room from the individual war rooms of the three services and was then plotted on the maps, with important news being passed on via Hollis and Ismay to the JPC, the Cabinet offices in Richmond Terrace and to Buckingham Palace: it is striking to see how the King's right to be kept informed was punctiliously observed. The plotters were required to prepare a summary for the Chiefs of Staff by 9 a.m. each day and helped the JPC with writing reports. Access to the Map Room was limited, that October, to forty-six persons: the War Cabinet and two other ministers, Sir Horace Wilson, the COS, the DCOS, the JPC staff of nine, six permanent military representatives and their staffs, and thirteen of the War Cabinet secretariat.[12]

The number of staff working in the War Rooms, whose name was changed in December from Central War Rooms to Cabinet War Rooms, had grown steadily. The secretarial and clerical staffs came from the Cabinet Office and Ismay's Military secretariat, and a number of messengers were also posted to the CWR. The need for security led to two NCOs and eight Royal Marine pensioners coming in as orderlies, and a Marine detachment provided guards for the external entrances. There were two of these until the King Charles Street door was closed, leaving only the entrance from St James's Park (now an entrance to the Treasury) and an internal approach along a corridor from Great George Street. In overall charge of security was Captain Adams, a Royal Marine.

The Standing Ministerial Committee on Military Coordination, set up in October 1939 under the chairmanship of Lord Chatfield with the three service ministers and the minister of supply as members, was not a success. A minister for the coordination of defence without executive authority had always been an anomaly, and in April 1940 Chamberlain asked for Chatfield's resignation and made Winston Churchill the committee's chairman, though the appointment of the first lord of the Admiralty was unlikely to be welcomed by either the other service ministers or, indeed, by their uniformed colleagues.

Interservice disagreements were a perennial problem. Ismay has recorded that, far from the Chiefs of Staff Committee exercising responsibility as a 'Battle Headquarters' for such matters as selecting commanders, issuing directives and instructions to commanders and receiving their reports:

> The Chief of the Naval Staff and the Chief of the Imperial General Staff acted with sturdy independence. They appointed their respective commanders without consultation with each other; and, worse still, they gave directives to these commanders without harmonising them. Thereafter they continued to give separate orders to them.[13]

As for the RAF, Air Marshal Arthur Barratt, the commander of the 'Advanced Air Striking Force' in France, was not only independent of General Lord Gort, commander-in-chief of the BEF, and of the French High Command, but received his orders direct from the commander-in-chief of Bomber Command in England. Ismay, after discussions with Barratt on a visit to British forces in France, emerged with the impression that the Air Staff 'would prefer to have their forces under Beelzebub than anyone connected with the Army'.[14]

Any vain hopes that Churchill, who had spent most of the interwar years out of office but was now back from the wilderness with a vengeance, would confine himself to Admiralty matters was soon confounded. He deluged Chamberlain with missives on everything from the need to bomb Germany, through the detailed equipment of the army in France, to the urgent need to reshuffle the government. As first lord, he was dynamic but rash. His plan to send a naval force to the Baltic was reminiscent of Admiral Fisher's proposal before the First World War: risky then but, without fighter cover, suicidal in 1939–40. It horrified Admiral Pound, who managed to squash it.

Churchill's chairmanship of the Ministerial Coordination Committee began just as the 'Bore War' became a hot war with Germany's invasion of Norway and Denmark in early April 1940. As first lord, he had already been pressing for operations in Norway and Sweden, with a view to cutting off Germany's supply of Swedish iron ore (transported by rail to the Norwegian port of Narvik), having directed the mining of Norwegian territorial waters which actually preceded the German attack. He dominated the subsequent ill-starred campaign in Norway, where British, French and Polish troops, often poorly prepared for a testing environment, were landed in Norway in the face of German air power. His chairmanship of the committee was not a success, and his determination to get his own way produced such chaos that Ismay had to 'implore the service chiefs to keep their tempers' and there was 'every chance of a first class row'.[15] John Colville recorded in his diary that, 'as was shown when Winston presided over the Military Coordination Committee, his verbosity and recklessness make a great deal of unnecessary work, prevented any real practical planning to be done and generally cause friction.'[16]

Churchill prided himself on his knowledge of military matters and this often led him to contradict or overrule senior officers. They naturally resented this, especially as doubts about his judgement and fears of his impulsiveness had been widespread since the Dardanelles campaign of 1915. Confronted by the alarming deterioration of relations between Churchill and the committee he chaired, Chamberlain took over himself on 16 April. On 24 April, Churchill told Chamberlain that he wanted to be minister of defence, a surprising demand in view of his handling of the Military Coordination Committee and his considerable share of the responsibility for the failure of the Norway campaign. A compromise was arranged whereby Churchill would chair the Military Coordination Committee in Chamberlain's absence and would also be responsible for giving 'guidance and direction to the Chiefs of Staff Committee with the power to summon them if necessary'. He was to be assisted by a 'Central Staff' under Ismay, who was to become a member of the Chiefs of Staff Committee.

Even Ismay, an admirer of Churchill, commented that 'these arrangements seemed rather odd'. There was already the military wing of the War Cabinet Secretariat, so what would be the role of the new Central Staff? Would Churchill really have the power to give guidance and direction, or would he only be able to give such guidance as the Committee approved? It became clear that Churchill expected Ismay to move into an office next to him in the Admiralty and had already decided that the 'Central Staff' would consist of a group of his close associates: 'Oliver Lyttelton for supply problems, (retired Major) Desmond Morton on the political side, and Professor Lindemann for scientific research and statistical work, and so forth.'[17] This put Ismay in an awkward position for, though he was eager to work under Churchill, he was loyal to his own military secretariat and he was reminded of Lloyd George's 'Garden Suburb', his special staff based in the grounds of 10 Downing Street, which had caused such friction with all government departments in an earlier war. Events were, however, moving swiftly, and the end of the Chamberlain government was very near.

It is one of the ironies of history that Churchill, who bore considerable responsibility for the Norwegian campaign, should have benefited from profound discontent with its failure. Disaster in Norway was, however, the proximate rather than the fundamental cause of Chamberlain's resignation. A man who rather despised charisma and fine words, he hated war and had, in all conscience, done his very best to avoid it, but he was not an inspiring leader when it came. He had done more to prepare Britain for war than was recognised for many years, and his strategy for defeating Germany seemed sensible enough: fight a defensive war alongside the French army, which many believed to be the best in the world, while the Royal Navy imposes a blockade that would deny Germany essential supplies, and the British and French economies steadily out-perform the German. However, both the main planks of this strategy soon splintered: the Nazi–Soviet Pact severely limited the effects of the blockade while the French army, flawed by the divisions in French society and, in its way, still haunted by the events of 1914–18, was about to implode.

Opinion polls were then in their infancy, but they suggest that Chamberlain enjoyed widespread popular support as late as March 1940. [18] It was not public opinion but a section of the elite, a minority of Conservative MPs, who abstained or voted against the government in the debate over the Norwegian campaign. After winning the vote of confidence but with such a drastically reduced majority that it was clear that he could not go on, Chamberlain resigned on 10 May 1940.

It was far from certain that Churchill would succeed him, though Lord Halifax, the preferred candidate in the eyes of many, wisely recognised that the country could not be led from the House of Lords. Churchill was mistrusted by many MPs, civil servants and generals but had the bearing of a war leader, was wholly determined and could inspire not just Parliament but a demoralised country. If he had the capacity to irritate, even infuriate, those who worked closely with him, he could also command the loyalty of many of those who had previously opposed him. 'Jock' Colville may stand as an example. An assistant private secretary to Chamberlain, whom he admired, he raised a glass to the fallen leader with Lord Dunglass, R. A. Butler and 'Chips' Channon after Chamberlain's resignation. He went shopping a few days after Churchill became prime minister, and bought:

> ... a bright blue new suit from the Fifty-Shilling Tailors, cheap and sensational looking, which I felt was appropriate to the new Government. But of

> course it must be admitted that Winston's administration, with all its faults, has drive.[19]

Colville stayed on under the new regime and soon Churchill had no greater admirer, though Colville never lost the ability to criticise his master.

Nevertheless, many of those who walked the corridors of power were aghast at the change. Lord Hankey thought Chamberlain 'well nigh indispensable' while Churchill, in contrast, was 'not 100 per cent reliable'. Sir Alexander Cadogan thought Churchill 'rambling and romantic and sentimental and temperamental', while General Sir John Dill, appointed CIGS by the new prime minister, thought him simply a 'nuisance'.[20] Many politicians, senior civil servants and high-ranking officers would take a year to reconcile themselves to Churchill.[21]

The new regime: Churchill in power

Churchill was fortunate in that he came to power just as the mood of the country was changing. Defeat in France, which proceeded apace in his first month in office, was discouraging, but the successful evacuation of much of the BEF from Dunkirk sparked a glimmer of hope. For a nation which was both fearful and stubborn, Churchill, with his bellicosity, showmanship and visible determination, was able to steady morale. Above all he imparted a new sense of urgency. The famous Low cartoon *All Behind You Winston*, which appeared in the *Evening Standard* on 14 May, 1940, depicts Churchill followed by members of his Cabinet and a mass of the general public with jackets off and sleeves rolled up. It captures the idea of a new start, a new urgency, a new unity and a new leader. The picture may have exaggerated the change in national mood, but change there undoubtedly was.

The new War Cabinet was a compromise. Its five members comprised Churchill himself, Labour party leader Clement Attlee and his deputy Arthur Greenwood (for this was a coalition government) Chamberlain (Conservative leader until, terminally ill, he resigned through ill-health) and Halifax (for the support of the majority of the Conservative Party was essential). Although the service ministers were not members, they regularly attended War Cabinet meetings, as did their chiefs of staff, while ministers whose departments were involved in subjects under discussion also attended when necessary. The role of the secretariat was crucial in underpinning the War Cabinet's deliberations and actions. Sir Edward Bridges, as secretary, attended all meetings and Ismay, as deputy secretary (military), the increasing number of meetings involving military matters. At least two assistant secretaries were usually also present.

Churchill combined the position of defence minister with that of prime minister. This made him almost a civilian 'generalissimo' in charge of the military part of the War Cabinet secretariat headed by Ismay, now a major-general, who became chief of staff to the minister of defence and a member of the Chiefs of Staff Committee. The Military Coordination Committee was evidently superfluous and was replaced by the Defence Committee headed by Churchill. This sub-divided into two committees dealing with operations and supply respectively. The prime minister was thus able to supervise the conduct of the war not just in terms of grand strategy but also with regard to the conduct of operations. He was able to summon the chiefs to the War Cabinet, to influence, via Ismay, the deliberations of the chiefs in their own committee and, by virtue of his chairmanship of the Defence Committee (Operations), directly to supervise military decisions. He was in control of the military to a far greater degree than Lloyd George had been in the First World War.

The counterpart to the Defence Committee, and indeed to Churchill's control of strategy and operations, was the Lord President's Committee, chaired first by Neville Chamberlain, then by Sir John Anderson and lastly by Clement Attlee, which was responsible for almost everything concerned with the Home Front. One downside to the prime minister's almost total command of the military side of the war was that he had to leave not only vital matters like economic policy and food but domestic policy in general to others. Another problem was that the new structure enabled Churchill, whose hands-on approach had been inclined to cause difficulties in the past, to involve himself far more in the detailed conduct of operations than was wise, and to embark upon ventures (the dispatch of troops to Greece in 1941 is a classic case in point) which appalled many of his professional advisers. However supportive of Churchill this author might be, no study of the higher conduct of the war can ignore the fact that he was often wrong, and only the industry and moral courage of his senior military associates, men like Ismay and Brooke, prevented some of his wilder notions from coming to fruition. The new system looked very much like an autocracy, but it was autocracy tempered by resolutely delivered advice.

Members of the defence secretariat had been apprehensive that it might be swept away as Churchill brandished the new broom. Ismay had certainly feared this some weeks previously, when Churchill had been made chairman of the Military Coordination Committee. 'Pug' Ismay was probably crucial to Churchill's decision to retain the services of the old CID secretariat, now the military secretariat of the War Cabinet. There was no defence department, so the secretariat effectively fulfilled this role. Ismay had long admired Churchill, and Churchill took to him from their first meeting. Ismay was a man whom almost everyone seems to have spoken well of: his influence was considerable, and his importance has often been underestimated. He described his role as being Churchill's 'agent' and 'my chief's shadow' but he was also a buffer between Churchill and the chiefs of staff. A supremely tactful man and a deft smoother of the many feathers left ruffled in Churchill's wake, Ismay was a crucially important figure, a veritable khaki eminence. The man who sets the agenda and writes up the minutes of a meeting is, notoriously, able to influence their content. Ismay wrote report after report, boiling down complex and often angry discussions, and was, as he put it, in the 'middle of the web'. He was unfailingly courteous and friendly not just to generals and politicians but to junior officers, clerks and secretaries. His natural flair for soothing may well have accompanied a shrewd concern for his own position, and his sunny view of the War Cabinet as 'a band of brothers' may be somewhat overdrawn. But, without him, relations between the War Rooms' principal inhabitants would have been much more antagonistic.

Ismay could perhaps afford that moral courage, so useful in his job, better than most, for a series of inheritances in the 1930s had left his wife wealthy and, as Ronald Lewin observed, 'independence of means ... increased his value as an objective adviser freed from the restrictions of an officer *de carrière*. He was, indeed, the "admirable Ismay".'

Under Major-General Ismay in the defence secretariat hierarchy came Colonel Leslie ('Jo') Hollis, looking after the operations side, and Colonel Ian Jacob, who was responsible for the supply committees. There were also about eight assistant military secretaries drawn from all three services. The major committees continued to be the Joint Planning Committee and the Joint Intelligence Committee, but as the war continued, committees, or more accurately Joint Staffs, each with its acronym, multiplied: the Strategic Planning Staff (STRATS), the Executive Planning Staff (EPS) and the Future Operational Staff (FOPS), along with committees for procurement, manpower and different aspects of supply, while the Joint Intelligence Staff also established numerous new committees.

The War Rooms were already becoming very crowded as these new staffs demanded space, and further demands were soon to be made of them. Ismay's concern that Churchill might replace the defence secretariat with his own body of advisers had proved groundless, but the prime minister's tight personal control of the war meant that his private secretaries became very much part of the team and were in daily contact with members of the defence secretariat. They were a relatively young group, consisting in 1940 of Anthony Bevir (44) and John Colville (25) who, as we have seen, had previously worked for Chamberlain, Eric Seal (42) and John Peck (27) who came with Churchill from the Admiralty, and John Martin (36) who had previously been with the Colonial Office and who became the principal private secretary in 1941 when Eric Seal was sent on a special mission to the USA. There was the vastly experienced Edith Watson, who was almost part of the fittings: 'If she had a departmental origin, nobody could remember what it was, for she had sat in Downing Street since the days of Lloyd George and Bonar Law' and had been promoted to private secretary.[22] Leslie Rowan joined as another private secretary in May 1941.

Then there were the prime minister's personal friends and trusted advisers, his 'kitchen cabinet': Brendan Bracken, his parliamentary private secretary from 1940–41,[23] Professor Frederick Lindemann, his scientific adviser, and Desmond Morton, his liaison officer with the intelligence services. Another old friend, the newspaper proprietor Lord Beaverbrook, was made minister for aircraft production in May and became a member of the War Cabinet in August.

At first Churchill made considerable use of the Defence Committee of the War Cabinet, which consisted of Attlee, Beaverbrook and the three service ministers, but gradually he summoned it less and less, and instituted a much more personal direction of the war. As he wrote: 'These formal meetings got fewer after 1941. As the machine began to work more smoothly I came to the conclusion that the daily meetings of the War Cabinet with the Chiefs of Staff were no longer necessary.'[24] With the Defence Committee gradually eclipsed, the direction of the war came increasingly to be in the hands of the prime minister and the Chiefs of Staff Committee. The Chiefs' Committee met separately every morning but Hollis's presence ensured that Churchill's case was always made, and in any event the prime minister frequently called in the chiefs. During the First World War, Lloyd George often found himself in conflict with his military advisers but, a generation later, the close proximity and daily contact between the prime minister and the chiefs ensured that, even if relations were not always harmonious, the chiefs respected the prime minister's authority and he, albeit sometimes reluctantly, would take their advice. Yet it could not really be called a 'system' of war management for it was hugely personal and idiosyncratic. Averell Harriman, a US special envoy, commented in 1941 that in Britain 'It was the politicians who ran the war ... not the generals and admirals'.[25] This was true in the sense that Churchill's authority was derived from Parliament, but to a very great extent it was just one forceful politician who ran the war.

Shortly after becoming prime minister, Churchill, visiting the underground Cabinet Room, announced, with characteristic gusto: 'This is the room from which I'll direct the war.' In fact, he was reluctant to go underground, not from fear of entrapment or claustrophobia but because to do so seemed a recognition of the enemy's strength, and was wholly contrary to his nature. Even during air-raids, he was fond of going up to the roofs of Whitehall buildings to see what was afoot. He preferred, before bombing raids on London began, to have conferences at the Admiralty or 10 Downing Street and, even during the Blitz, to have daytime meetings elsewhere and only attend evening meetings in the underground Cabinet Room. He recognised, however, the crucial importance of having a headquarters where key staff, the central nervous system of the war, could work in comparative security, with a high degree of secrecy and good communications.

The first months of the Churchill government saw little in the way of air attacks on Britain. The War Cabinet met in the War Room on 29 July but held no further meetings there until the Blitz began in September. Nevertheless, the already pressing demands for more space increased from May onwards and became heavier from September. The need for better facilities, more protection and greater space was already obvious, but a new urgency came with the summer and autumn of 1940.

There have been no more desperate or dramatic months in modern British history than those which followed Churchill's succession to the premiership. The swastika was fluttering over Amsterdam, Brussels and Paris, and Britain's options were limited. On 2 July Hitler ordered work to start on plans for the invasion of Britain, and on 19 July he made a speech in the Reichstag offering peace to the British. The terms on offer would have amounted to an acceptance of German hegemony over most of Europe. Britain could either accept them or face the threat of invasion with little hope of eventual victory in the absence of any continental ally.

In a sense Churchill's answer had already been given when, on 3 July, he had ordered an attack on the French fleet anchored at Oran in French North Africa, fearing that it might fall into German hands. This brutally realistic act affirmed Britain's determination to continue the war, making it clear to the Americans that Churchill would brook no compromises. It also underlined the importance of Britain's naval superiority over Germany, which constitutes, along with the RAF's magnificent victory in the Battle of Britain and the evacuation of substantial forces from Dunkirk, one of the three main reasons for Britain's survival in what were, by any reasonable measure, its darkest days. There were Cabinet discussions over the possibilities of peace but it is clear that the prime minister, if unable to prevent such debate, ensured that no serious thought was given to any possible agreement with the Germans. Although his natural optimism was tempered by periods of fretting, most notably about the submarine menace, he looked to national spirit and ethos, and sought comfort in the history of previous occasions when Britain had seemed close to disaster. However, he admitted to his niece, Clarissa Churchill, that there was 'just a chance' that Britain could actually pull through.

The summer and autumn of 1940, which Churchill himself styled Britain's 'finest hour', are an extraordinary example of a charismatic leader's ability to transmit his resolution to a nation. Churchill said later that it was the British people that had the lion's heart: all he provided was the roar. This is an underestimation of his role for he used words to inspire confidence, mobilising the language of Shakespeare, it was said, and sending it into battle. His oratory, apparently effortlessly delivered but prepared, as we now know, with infinite care, went straight to the nation's heart. As historian Paul Addison has written: 'At some point between May 1940 and the London blitz of September, the career of Winston Churchill merged into the history of the British people.'[26]

Churchill was demanding. Although he was sixty-five when he came to power, he did not spare himself – and saw no reason to spare others – long hours and lost weekends. He demanded unrealistically rapid responses to questions, whole-hearted effort and efficiency: 'respectable civil servants were actually to be seen running along the corridors.'[27] His personal staff, the defence secretariat and the chiefs of staff were expected to be either in session or on call. His demands were often unreasonable and were sometimes resented, but he was quickly forgiven, partly because of awareness of the common crisis but, partly too, because of the loyalty he commanded.

Relations between the chiefs of staff and a prime minister who considered himself an expert on strategy and military operations were bound to be difficult. Britain had no senior commander quite like the US Admiral Ernest King, who believed that civilians should 'be told nothing of the war until it ended, and then only who had won', but, though senior British commanders fully accepted the right of the prime minister and the Cabinet to make major strategic decisions with the aid of military advice, they believed that they should otherwise be free from civilian interference.

Churchill felt that dash and determination were

the secrets of success, while most senior officers had come to believe that superiority in men and weaponry was the crucial factor. The one thing the prime minister had in common with Hitler was a belief in the triumph of the will. He found too many of his generals to be conservative and over-cautious. The chiefs, for their part, were horrified by Churchill's enthusiasm for minor assaults on occupied Europe, which they thought would accomplish little at considerable cost, by his failure to understand the necessity for air cover for both naval and army operations, and by his innate affection for swashbuckling and glamorous commanders, whether, like Field Marshal Sir Harold Alexander, they were brave and charming but strategically lightweight or, like Major-General Orde Wingate of Chindit fame, possessed Biblical zeal laced with remarkable eccentricity.

In May, the CIGS, General Ironside, who had generally been felt not to have been a success, was replaced by General Sir John Dill. Perhaps surprisingly, Ironside then became commander-in-chief of Home Forces,[28] probably the most crucial post at a time when invasion was expected. Dill, hitherto vice-CIGS and so a natural candidate for top job in the army, was personally able, had great social skills and was responsible for the efficient reorganisation of the army's high command. But it soon became clear that Churchill found him dull and uninspiring, nicknaming him 'Dilly Dally'. Alan Brooke, coming back from an exercise in Dill's car in November 1940, thought him depressed: 'He finds the PM very difficult to deal with.' Looking back years later, he commented that 'it would have been impossible for those two men to hit it off together'.[29]Admiral

Sir Dudley Pound found the perfect answer to some of the prime minister's wilder schemes in agreeing with them and then allowing evidence of their impracticability to accumulate. In October, at the time of a Cabinet reshuffle, Colville expected a purge of the chiefs of staff, 'who are sound but old and slow',[30] but it was only Newall who went, being replaced as chief of Air Staff by Sir Charles Portal. All the tact of Ismay and Bridges was required to keep relations between Churchill and the chiefs relatively harmonious.

Britain's naval supremacy and her victory in the Battle of Britain eventually led to Hitler calling off his invasion plan, Operation 'Sea Lion'. Historians still debate the genuine feasibility of cross-channel invasion, but the threat seemed very real until the attack on Russia in June 1941 gave Germany other priorities. Clarissa Churchill, later the wife of Anthony Eden, recalled finding, many years later, a large capsule, much discoloured by age, in a drawer, She showed it to her husband, who said it was 'his cyanide pill' which he and Churchill had been given in case they were captured.[31]

Even before the intensive bombing, nicknamed the Blitz, began on 7 September, there were yet more demands on the space of the War Rooms. The prime minister and War Cabinet might be content to stay in their usual offices for the moment, but arrangements had to be made for moves when the expected air-raids started. In May, Hollis observed that if the prime minister moved into the War Rooms his staff would come with him, taking up a lot of space. On 27 July, Room 65A was set aside as a personal office and bedroom for Churchill and it became his emergency accommodation. This room had previously been set aside for War Cabinet meetings but a larger room, 69, at the northern end of the basement corridor and previously an Office of Works shelter, had been found for this purpose in September 1939. Churchill's immediate staff, consisting of Ismay and three of his private secretaries, were allocated rooms (66, 66A and 66B) which had previously been the strongrooms of the Office of Works. Room 64, next to the Map Room (65), became its annexe. There was insufficient space, and the Joint Planners, whose numbers grew, had to lead a peripatetic existence using whatever rooms were vacant at any time.

The problem of insufficient space increased enormously when the chiefs of staff decided at the end of May that an Advanced Headquarters of the Home Defence Executive should be installed in the Cabinet War Rooms. This body had been created in haste as the threat of invasion loomed.

General Headquarters Home Forces, directly responsible for defence against invasion, had at first been based at Kneller Hall in Twickenham and then moved to St Paul's School in Hammersmith, but the urgent circumstances suggested that its commander needed to be close to the prime minister: this was very much a mixed blessing in the view of General Brooke, who became commander-in-chief of Home Forces in July. The War Rooms, with their good communications, were the obvious place from which to conduct the first phase of the defence of Britain if invasion came. The arrival of Home Forces' staff caused great difficulties as they surged into the whole place. They were allocated several rooms on the main corridor, occupied six rooms in the basement and their

Advanced Signals Section and Intelligence and Operations clerks moved into the Dock, the very lowest section of the War Rooms. The situation was eased when Advanced HQ eventually moved to join the rest of GHQ Home Forces, which was by then in the basement and sub-basement under the large West Court of the NPO in January 1941.

The CWR expanded 'vertically into the sub-ground level and the Dock [the cellar below the basement], and later horizontally, into rooms under the Western Courtyards of the NPO'.[32] The Blitz made everyone conscious of the flimsiness of many Whitehall buildings and the relative strength of the solidly built early twentieth-century NPO, and departments less involved in running the war were gradually eased out and central and defence staff moved in until the whole building effectively became a war headquarters, with the CWR in the basement as its citadel.

Churchill was predictably reluctant to leave No. 10 Downing Street, and it took real bombing rather than merely its threat to make him move out. The great raids on London started in early September, and though London's docklands and East End got the worst of the Blitz, nowhere was safe and the centres of government were obvious targets. On the night of 12 September, Whitehall was hit and the Ministry of Transport damaged. Because of this the War Cabinet decided to meet in the underground War Room on the following day. During the meeting a message was handed to Churchill, telling him that Buckingham Palace had been dive-bombed: King George VI suspected that he had been under family-fire from a relative serving in an enemy air force.[33]

No. 10 Downing Street was a vulnerable old building. A shelter was built in the garden and a dining room and sitting room set up in the basement, and while this work was going on Churchill stayed for a while in the Carlton Hotel in nearby Belgravia. It was decided, however, that No. 10 was still too dangerous for the prime minister to continue to use it as a permanent residence. John Colville recorded in his diary on 16 September:

> At No. 10 there is a certain chaos caused by the fact that the building is said to be unsafe. The basement is being fitted up for the PM to live and work in, and meanwhile much of the time, both by day and by night, is being spent in the disagreeable atmosphere of the Central War Room.[34]

Churchill spent the nights of the 16th and 18th there, two of the few nights he was to sleep in the CWR during the whole of the war: he was more commonly to be found in his flat in the No. 10 Annexe in the NPO itself, above ground but in close contact with what he regarded as the war's nerve-centre. That September most of his personal staff slept in the shelter under No. 10, but it was clear that the prime minister, the War Cabinet and their key personnel would have to move to safer accommodation, though it was by no means certain that the underground War Rooms would become their base. The newly constructed Church House in Westminster, very close to Westminster Abbey (in use as a conference centre at the time of writing), was suggested as a stronger building for Churchill and his personal staff: the hoary old question of whether to stay in Whitehall or to move to Dollis Hill arose again, this time as a matter of urgency. Other options included concrete rotundas in Horseferry Road (code named 'Anson'), Montagu House, the Faraday Building and Curzon House, all reinforced buildings reasonably close to Whitehall and already earmarked for essential staff. There were also plans to turn Dover Street Underground Station (now Green Park Station) into a citadel.

Churchill had agreed on 14 September to plans for the evacuation of senior civil servants and ministers and thought that these might have to be implemented fairly soon, envisioning 600 people moving within six hours, but on the 16th he decided that 'the time has not yet come to move'. On 20 September, Colville accompanied Mr and Mrs Churchill to an inspection of the Cabinet's emergency headquarters at Dollis Hill (code-named 'Paddock'), the flats where they would live, and

> The deep underground rooms safe from the biggest bomb, where the Cabinet and its satellites (e.g. me) would work and, if necessary sleep. They are impressive but rather forbidding; I suppose if the present intensive bombing continues we must get used to being troglodytes ('trogs' as the PM puts it). I begin to understand what the early Christians must have felt about living in the Catacombs.[35]

Never one to waste a phrase he had coined, next day Churchill wrote to Chamberlain: 'I propose to lead a troglodyte existence with several "trogs".'

By mid-September arrangements began for

Churchill's working headquarters to be transferred to the No. 10 Annexe, specially prepared rooms in the NPO above the underground War Rooms. The Churchills finally moved there in December 1940, and the prime minister and his wife were to live there until the end of the war, but he continued to spend the daylight hours at No. 10 and often passed the night at the London Underground's offices at the former Down Street Underground Station while the No. 10 Annexe was being prepared. The station had been on the Piccadilly Line between Dover Street and Hyde Park Corner, but, never busy, it had been closed in 1932. The platform faces had been bricked up and the resulting space made a large bunker, whose main occupant was now the Emergency Railway Committee. It was not only safe, if somewhat noisy because of the underground rattling past only a wall away, but comfortable, with a dining room where the food was considered to be excellent. As well as Churchill himself, Cabinet ministers and senior civil servants made use of it.

Before he moved into the No. 10 Annexe in the NPO, the prime minister had the choice of a number of places where he could spend the night, and his staff had great difficulty keeping track of his movements, especially as he often changed his mind. This, together with Churchill's habit of labelling urgent messages for 'Action This Day' and his fondness for beginning sentences with 'Pray ...', occasioned a mock minute from a private secretary, John Peck:

> ACTION THIS DAY
>
> Pray let six new offices be fitted for my use, in Selfridge's, Lambeth Palace, Stanmore, Tooting Bec, the Palladium and Mile End Road. I will inform you at 6 each evening at which office I shall dine work and sleep. Accommodation will be required for Mrs Churchill, two shorthand-typists, three secretaries and Nelson [No. 10's black cat which Churchill was very fond of]. There should be a shelter for all and a place for me to watch air-raids from the roof. This should be completed by Monday. There is to be no hammering during office hours, that is between 7 a.m. and 3 a.m.
>
> W.S.C.
>
> 31. 10. 40.[36]

That Morton, Jacob, Seal, Ismay and others were, so Colville tells us, convinced that this minute was authentic, tells us much about what Churchill's staff had to put up with.

On 3 October, the prime minister, the War Cabinet and the chiefs of staff all went for a trial day at the NPO. The rooms at the No. 10 Annexe were by no means bomb-proof but the building was much sturdier than No. 10 itself and had steel shutters, which could be closed during air-raids, over its windows. The prime minister and his wife had a ground-floor flat made up of two rooms formerly used by government typists. The situation remained fluid, however, and the option of Dollis Hill remained open. By October, Churchill had decided that the War Cabinet and the secretariat would stay in Whitehall, at least for the time being. No. 10 Downing Street remained furnished and the Cabinet Room was available for meetings, but the central direction of the war was henceforth to be conducted from the NPO. The floor above the underground CWR became the No. 10 Annexe and there followed an expansion of the 'Battle Headquarters' into other parts of the building. Too fine a distinction should not be made between these various locations, for all were part of the web of the War Cabinet, its civil and military secretariats and the expanding number of sections and committees they spawned. The underground War Rooms remained, however, the innermost sanctum and the safest place for the War Cabinet and chiefs of staff to meet when there was a bombing raid.

But how safe was this 'Battle Headquarters'? Until February 1941, the Luftwaffe had made 40 attacks on Whitehall but only 146 heavy explosive bombs had fallen within 1,000 yards of the Cenotaph in Whitehall. Germany's failure to invest in long-range aircraft capable of carrying heavy bombs severely limited the damage caused by the Blitz. Nevertheless, the danger of a direct hit on the War Rooms was real and Churchill was startled when he discovered they were not really protected against such an occurrence and gave orders that they should be reinforced. This led to the War Cabinet formally deciding, on 22 October 1940, that further protection should be provided. It took the form of a layer of three to four feet of concrete reinforced with two layers of rails above the War Rooms. Thus began the saga of what Burgis called the 'never-ending Slab', which was gradually extended to cover both the War Rooms themselves and the adjacent rooms below the NPO's courtyards. The Air Ministry, which occupied some other parts of the building, promptly demanded a concrete lid over the King Charles Street front and over the basement rooms where Flying Operations HQ was located. By the end of 1940, the Slab covered the area beneath the courts beyond the existing War Rooms. It also protected the larger West Court basement near the centre of the NPO, where the operational headquarters of Home Forces had moved on its departure from the original War Rooms.

The War Rooms might now seem to be reasonably well defended, but as the war progressed the Germans produced ever more powerful bombs and it was again suggested that the rooms were vulnerable. In 1943, it was decided that no further protection could reasonably be provided and that if bombing raids were resumed then the prime minister would have to sleep elsewhere and lesser inhabitants would have to take their chances with the existing protection.

While the issue of protection was, happily, never put to the test, overcrowding was a major practical problem. Despite the evacuation of hundreds of civil servants from Whitehall, there was a shortage of space in government offices. Running the war may indeed have required a complex administration, but the civilian and military bureaucracy had an inbuilt impetus to growth. New organisations and departments proliferated and then acquired subsidiaries. Even – or perhaps especially – in times of crisis, our territorial instincts dictate that organisations and departments fight for space, and promotion and status are closely associated with their expansion. Importance and influence seemed to be proportionate to closeness to the centre of things: and the centre was the prime minister, the War Cabinet and the chiefs of staff. No department wanted to be exiled to Horseferry Road or Montagu House. A turf war for rooms in the NPO took place. The Office of Works fiercely resented losing space, the Treasury and the Ministry of Health resisted eviction, and the Air Ministry fought tooth and nail for accommodation.

As well as the danger that bombing posed to the War Rooms, there was another serious concern. It had been suggested in October 1939 that the Germans might assault Whitehall with airborne troops. Churchill appears to have taken this possibility very seriously and in May 1940 ordered CinC Home Forces to report on safeguards against it, and a company of Local Defence Volunteers (later the Home Guard) was allocated to Whitehall. There was, it transpired, little coordination of those forces that were in Whitehall as each building had its own little garrison. There were men of the Grenadier Guards at the War Office, Royal Marines at the Admiralty and airmen at the Air Ministry, while other departments had Local Defence Units. GHQ Home Forces and the Westminster Garrison Command were inclined to allow each sector to prepare its own plan of defence under the loose supervision of an overall commander. The Home Guard was dissatisfied with the lack of a unified command and with poor coordination between Home Guard and regular forces. Ismay arranged for GHQ Home Forces to appoint an overall commander for the defence of Whitehall, and his authority was established.

In July, Churchill thought that an attack was very likely and a new defence scheme was drawn up. There was to be a detachment of Grenadier Guards, with its commanding officer, two more officers and 158 other ranks, with a headquarters in Horse Guards, supported by Marines in the Admiralty and by the Home Guard. It was thought that the Life Guards could provide additional reinforcement from their Knightsbridge barracks. Sentry posts and roadblocks were set up, and a barbed wire entanglement was placed in St James's Park. GHQ Home Forces organised mobile detachments, each of about 250 men, to support the Whitehall garrison in the event of a surprise attack.

The War Room had its own arrangements, with the Royal Marine orderlies and guards supported by twelve Grenadiers, known as 'Rance's Guard', on duty at the main entrance. Within the War Rooms, the defence plan was for the camp commandant or Map Room duty officer to assume command if there was an attack and to organise Map Room and Joint Planning Staff as a reserve to the Royal Marines guarding the entrance. There was also a 'Fortress Commander' for the NPO as a whole. Any German attack would have undoubtedly had to deal with Churchill in person, unless his aides had held him back forcibly. Lawrence Burgis commented in his diary that, if Britain had in fact been invaded, the prime minister 'would have mustered his Cabinet and died with them in the pill-box disguised as a WHSmith bookstall in Parliament Square'.[37] Indeed, he had already warned them that if the worst came to the worst, they would all finish up 'choking in our own blood on the ground'.

Even so, the defence arrangements for the NPO were still insufficiently coordinated and by January

1942 it appeared that although GHQ Home Forces had appointed a fortress commander, the Westminster garrison was still inclined to let each department in the building prepare its own plan. The matter was eventually resolved by the appointment of NPO Office Commandant, Sir Eric Crankshaw, as commandant of the NPO Fortress. Historian Nigel de Lee has commented that:

> The War Rooms took little active part in the NPO defence schemes. The primary role of War Room personnel was defence of their own location, assisted by Rance's Guard, who were drawn from a platoon of Grenadiers stationed inside the NPO.[38]

Whether an attack on Whitehall was ever likely is debatable. The JIC thought that large-scale assault by paratroops would have been very difficult considering the area's air defences, but thought there might be a surprise attack by a small number of troops with the aim of paralysing the centre of government, even though it would have been a suicidal venture. Probably the most dangerous place for the prime minister and his entourage was Chequers. Churchill made extensive use of this mansion near Aylesbury, in the Chilterns, the official country residence of prime ministers since 1921. It gave him the opportunity for weekends away from the hothouse atmosphere of Whitehall. If there was opportunity for relaxation, these were also working weekends with house parties composed of senior officers, advisers and ministers. An isolated country house in many ways offered an easier target for the Luftwaffe than any Whitehall building, and German intelligence must have known that Chequers was where Churchill and many of his staff were to be found at weekends. Aware of this, the prime minister, sometimes stayed at Ditchley Park, the home of the Conservative MP Ronald Tree and not far from Churchill's birthplace, Blenheim Palace, especially when there was a full moon, which made Chequers, with its easily visible drive, particularly vulnerable. There was also a possibility that the Germans would use paratroops or special forces to snatch or kill Churchill, and Chequers was provided with a military guard for his protection.

By the end of 1940, an invasion did not seem so likely, and Britain had survived for the time being. By now most of the central features of the headquarters that the NPO had become were in place, as were many of the individuals who would help Churchill direct Britain's war. The underground War Rooms were part of the complex within the NPO from which the war was directed. Known to cognoscenti as the 'Bunker' or the 'Hole', they were the most secure, but also the most uncomfortable, part of the headquarters. Churchill, his personal staff and advisers, the War Cabinet, the secretariat and the chiefs of staff much preferred to meet above ground but convened in the subterranean accommodation when bombing raids were expected, usually in the evenings.

The Blitz meant that from September 1940 until May 1941 and again in 1944, with the 'little Blitz' at the beginning of the year, and later when V1s and V2s posed a risk, there was extensive use of the bunker by the senior echelons but that in 1942 and 1943 this use declined sharply.[39] The permanent inhabitants of the War Rooms were those working in the Map Room, the Joint Planners, the Joint Intelligence Staff and all their support staff, the telephonists, typists and stenographers, and the marine orderlies and guards.

The senior staff of the military side of the War Cabinet secretariat would remain in their positions throughout the war. In theory the military assistant secretaries would come and go, and many were, indeed, eager to rejoin fighting units; but working in the CWR was a specialist occupation and it was found wasteful to have men who had acquired experience there move on to ships, regiments or squadrons, so there was, in practice, considerable continuity. Sir Edward Bridges remained in control of the secretariat as a whole throughout the war. Most practical work was done by his deputy director (civil), Sir Rupert Howarth, who retired in 1942 and was replaced first by Norman Brook, and, after Brook was promoted permanent secretary to the Ministry of Reconstruction in December 1943, by two under-secretaries, Sir Gilbert Laithwaite and W.S. Murrie.

Rather like Lloyd George's War Cabinet, Churchill's had expanded considerably from its original five members and by the end of 1940 it numbered eight. Beaverbrook arrived in August and Ernest Bevin, Minister of Labour and National Service, followed in October. As Bevin's appointment upset the party balance, the Conservative chancellor of the exchequer, Sir Kingsley Wood, became a member. Chamberlain, who had an operation for stomach cancer in July, effectively ceased to be a member thereafter, though he did not resign until 30 September, only a month before his death, and was replaced by the new lord president of the Council, Sir John Anderson. Anthony Eden, secretary of state for war, succeeded Lord Halifax as Foreign Secretary and member of the War Cabinet when Halifax, much against his will, was persuaded to become ambassador to Washington in December.

Among the chiefs of staff, Sir John Dill remained CIGS but was increasingly at odds with Churchill, Sir Dudley Pound was still first sea lord and Sir Charles Portal had replaced Sir Cyril Newall as chief of the Air Staff. General Alan Brooke was proving a dynamic CinC Home Forces and, when the prime minister was eventually to despair of Dill, 'Brookie' would be the obvious, if reluctant, replacement for a man he deeply admired.

Churchill's position had grown more powerful. There was still some resistance to him in Parliament but he became leader of the Conservative Party in October, which consolidated his position, and he enjoyed great popularity with the public. One of Churchill's largely positive contributions was his determination to bypass the slurry of bureaucracy and standard procedure. Among the negative features of Britain – even Britain at war – were the growth of managerialism, the sanctity of hierarchy and the dead hand of the rule book. During the First World War, Lloyd George had found it necessary to make changes and to employ 'men of push and go'. A generation later the urgencies of wartime once more made it necessary to harness the abilities of the unorthodox and the adventurous. Churchill was, at one and the same time, deeply conservative with a love of tradition and old institutions, but hugely impatient with conventions and rules if they stood in the way of action. The direction of the war now had a dynamism which came from a successful synthesis of his ebullient qualities and the professionalism and careful planning of the secretariat and the chiefs of staff. It was a heady and sometimes unstable mix, but it served Britain extremely well.

Although an embattled Britain had lasted through 1940, the question at the year's end was what she could do, with her limited resources, to go beyond mere survival. In previous wars, when hard-pressed, Britain had been able to rely upon a European ally, or at least the prospect of finding one, her control of the sea and the resources of her Empire. In the winter of 1940 the continent was shut off and, though the Dominions had rallied to the cause, only Canada would be able to bring her growing strength to bear on Western Europe, and even this would take time. Churchill, with his American mother and a deep affection for the United States which was not, as he put it, 'strangled by old school ties', genuinely believed that there was something special about the English-Speaking Peoples, and had persuaded Roosevelt to take him seriously. In March 1941, the Lend-Lease Act was to enable the USA to supply Britain with military equipment, but for the moment all Churchill could expect was tacit support. Churchill welcomed strategic bombing as the only way of striking Germany, and campaigning in North Africa offered, by the year's end, the prospect of doing serious damage to the Italians. But none of this was remotely war-winning stuff. In the winter of 1940–41, the denizens of the CWR, their atmosphere thick with cigarette smoke leavened by wafts from the chemical lavatories in the Dock, were conscious that this was a war where survival seemed more likely than victory. Not for nothing was Churchill's watchword 'KBO' – 'keep buggering on'. There seemed little else on the agenda.

3

RUNNING THE SHOW

From a purely British point of view, 1940, when the nation's very survival hung in the balance, was the most crucial year of the war. Despite our tendency to hyperbolise, Britain did not in fact stand alone, for she had support of the Empire and the Dominions. Nonetheless, after June, she lacked a continental ally and the sea lanes connecting her to the rest of the world were threatened by Germany's U-boats: her plight was precarious indeed.

A broader perspective suggests that 1941 has a greater claim to be termed the 'fulcrum of the twentieth century'. By the early summer, there were no longer constant bombing raids on London. This was, in part, recognition by the Luftwaffe that its loss of aircraft was not justified by the damage they inflicted, but was also an indication that Hitler was now turning his gaze to the east. Germany's invasion of the Soviet

Union that summer broadened a European war, providing Britain with an unlikely, though not wholly palatable, continental sword. At the very end of the year, Japan's attack upon Pearl Harbor, as well as upon the British Empire in the Far East and the headless colonies of France and the Netherlands, led, due to Hitler's almost incomprehensible decision to declare war on the USA, to the United States being at war not only with Japan but also with Germany. The conflict was now indeed a 'world war' or, more accurately (as there was little effective coordination between Japan and Germany, and until 1945 no fighting between Russia and Japan), two wars linked by the participation in both of Britain and the USA.

At the beginning of 1941, these developments could hardly have been guessed at. Germany and the Soviet Union seemed to be on the same good terms that had held since the Ribbentrop-Molotov Pact of 1939, President Roosevelt had just been re-elected on a platform of keeping the United States out of the war, and Japan appeared preoccupied with her own struggle in China though she was in fact preparing to move into French Indochina, Dutch Indonesia, and for subsequent war with Britain and the USA. Churchill, however, remained optimistic that America would eventually be persuaded to enter the conflict and, despite his genuine detestation of Communism, he hoped that those two totalitarian giants, Germany and the Soviet Union, would eventually fall out. For the time being, though, Britain's only real opportunity for waging war on land was to oppose Italy and uphold the British position in the Mediterranean and North Africa. Here the early successes of British forces under General Sir Archibald Wavell were followed by debacle when, at Churchill's behest, Britain sent forces that could not be spared from North Africa, to aid Greece, invaded by Germany in April. Greece was overrun and in May, after heavy fighting, the island of Crete, where many of the survivors of the Greek expedition had ended up, was taken by the Germans in a costly airborne assault. In a repeat of Dunkirk on a smaller scale, British and Commonwealth forces had to be evacuated, at great cost to the Royal Navy, upholding some of its finest traditions under repeated air attack. German troops had arrived in North Africa, under an unknown lieutenant general called Erwin Rommel, and proved far more formidable than their Italian allies. As the pendulum of war swung across the deserts of Egypt and Libya, Churchill's patience with his generals was to be sorely tried, and the CWR echoed to his strictures on weak and ineffective commanders.

A central command headquarters

The great concrete Slab crept over more and more of the basements of the NPO at the very time that the air-raids it was designed to protect against were declining in ferocity. January and February 1941 saw less frequent raids on London and, though the Luftwaffe returned in force during March and April, the raid of 10 May, the worst of the whole war, marked the end of the Blitz. Any doubts as to the need for increased protection of the CWR would have been confounded by this 'valedictory' raid, which killed 1,400 people, damaged Westminster Hall and gutted the House of Commons. The Slab, as we have seen, did not give complete defence against an armour-piercing bomb and Ian Jacob admitted that he always knew that the War Rooms were not bomb-proof, but, beneath several storeys of a steel-framed building, the Slab gave a fair degree of physical protection and was psychologically comforting. Such things never mattered to Churchill himself, but both protection and reassurance would become important once more in 1944.

Most of the central features of the NPO were in place by the spring of 1941. The Slab had permitted a considerable expansion of the underground rooms, which had now been extended to three times their original size. The new space under the Central Courtyard was taken up by the Churchills' dining room, a bedroom for Mrs Churchill, a kitchen, dining room and a reserve meeting room for the chiefs of staff. There were office/bedrooms for Churchill's advisers, private secretaries and War Cabinet ministers under Court 12; the southernmost group of rooms housed the telephone exchange, a first-aid room and a canteen; and a large complex of rooms (where the Churchill Museum is today) was used by the Joint Intelligence Staff and the Joint Planning Staff after Home Forces had moved out in 1942.

Many of the underground rooms duplicated those set aside for Churchill, his staff, advisers and family and the senior members of the secretariat in the ground and upper floors of the NPO and tended to be used only occasionally by them. The Cabinet Office was based both in the underground War Rooms and on the second floor and it was there that the senior members of the secretariat, Ismay, Hollis and Jacob, were located. James Leasor's assertion that 'Against the background hum of fans, pumping in filtered air from miles away, Hollis, Ismay and others worked for eighteen hours a day, week after week, month after month, year after year'[1] is an exaggeration so far as senior members of the secretariat were concerned. They certainly worked extremely hard, but generally did so above ground. General Jacob remembered that he occasionally attended meetings in the War Rooms, but actually worked on the second floor of the NPO, though he never called it that, terming it instead Great George Street. He would walk down into the Map Room on most evenings and have supper in the mess, where there was interesting company, and occasionally he slept down there. Churchill, he said, was found in the War Rooms occasionally after the start of the Blitz but later hardly used his bedroom, though he went down into the basement to growl out the words of so many of those broadcasts which helped keep Britain's hopes alive, and, from late 1941, to make his crucial transatlantic telephone calls.[2] Churchill did not actually live in the CWR, but he could scarcely have lived without them.

From December 1940, the No. 10 Annexe was the Churchills' main base. In February 1941, the prime minister invited General Brooke to see his new flat: 'we visited his study, sitting room, dining room, Mrs Churchill's bedroom, his room, kitchen, scullery etc!!' Brooke commented after the war that: 'He was just like a small boy showing his new toy and all that it could do! He certainly had been very comfortably fitted out, and was just above the War Cabinet Room, Map Rooms, Cabinet Staff, etc.'[3]

Despite his evident delight in his new quarters, Churchill still preferred No. 10 itself and during the daytime would spend as much time there as possible, with Cabinet meetings almost always being held there during the day and, after the bombing had become less severe, in the late evenings as well. Much of No. 10 remained furnished and in the spring of 1941 John Colville and Churchill's brother Jack used to sleep on the top floor in the bedrooms formerly used by the prime minister and his wife.[4] The prime minister, his staff and the secretariat lived a somewhat peripatetic existence, with the secretarial and kitchen staff never quite knowing whether meals or appointments for the day were to be held at No. 10 or in No. 10 Annexe in the NPO.

Elizabeth Nel, who became a secretary to Churchill in May 1941, wrote that, although he chaired evening Cabinet meetings in the War Rooms, Churchill then returned to the ground-level flat above them to finish off the evening in his study. She herself, after late nights spent taking dictation from the premier, would descend to the bedrooms below the War Rooms to snatch some sleep. She wrote of the War Rooms that 'Here some of the most brilliant British officers spent their days breathing conditioned air and working by daylight lamps, to emerge white-faced and blinking for a few hours in the evening.'[5]

Gladys Hymer, a secretary who was transferred to the Cabinet Office in May 1941, has described her first visit to the War Rooms. She passed a 'Marine on guard at the main entrance with fixed bayonet' and two floors underground found, under huge beams, a 'small room absolutely littered with paper – five or six typing tables and roneo machine, armchair and radio'. At first she had to work in a narrow corridor with low flood doors which she had to hop over. She sensed a feeling of great activity and 'saw a lot of coming and going of people like Smuts, Churchill, Mountbatten, Attlee and other members of Cabinet'. One of the typists' jobs was to go the Map Room every morning at 8 a.m. to collect the daily summary of everything that had happened during the previous twenty-four hours. This was typed up and copies were rolled off the duplicator as quickly as possible so as to be on the desks of high-ranking officers by 9 a.m. She describes the Map Room, manned twenty-four hours a day by service officers, the small mess where meals were prepared for senior staff at any time of day or night, Churchill's bedroom, Mrs Churchill's bedroom, 'where Mary [Churchill] often slept', the 'tiny phone room – with bolt showing vacant and engaged – like a Loo', the bedrooms for other high-ranking people and three rooms for the JPS, 'who were the only people who actually worked there all the time'.[6]

The Map Room was the heart of the CWR and the 'scoreboard' of the war. It is not surprising that senior officers and civil servants on the list of those allowed access often used to find excuses to drop in, for in this room was displayed the latest information on the worldwide state of the conflict. Much of it was relayed to the Map Room via the 'beauty chorus', the lines of coloured telephones linked to the Admiralty, the War Office, the Air Ministry and other key organisations; the telephones had flashing lights rather than bells and three were fitted with scramblers so that, if the wires were tapped, conversations would be incomprehensible. Here indeed was the world at war, graphically displayed on the maps which lined the walls: a large map of the world on one wall was speckled with pinned symbols denoting the position of warships and convoys. From June 1941, another map enabled the observer to see the positions of the German and Russian armies in eastern Europe and from December 1941 a further map depicted the extent of Japan's advance and then its retreat across the Pacific. General Ismay has written that:

> Whenever a big battle or critical movement was in progress, it was a temptation to find pretexts for going to the War Room at all hours of the day and night, in order to get the very latest information. The sensation was not unlike visiting a friend in hospital. One entered the room hoping for the best, but fearing the worst. 'How is the Malta convoy going?' one would ask, trying not to appear unduly anxious. The nature of the answer could generally be guessed from the expression of the officer on duty.[7]

Churchill had his own map room in No. 10 Annexe, which was maintained by Captain Richard Pim RNVR. Pim was a former Northern Ireland civil servant and the prime minister had brought him to No. 10 from the Admiralty. The contents of this map room were portable for, when the prime minister travelled to confer with allies, Pim would pack up his maps and then set them up in convenient rooms or the cabins of ships.

With so many officers dropping in to the Map Room, the adjacent Mess in Room 68 became very popular. Here there always seems to have been plenty to drink and it was only towards the very end of the war that a daily ration of two large whiskies and two large gins was introduced. Royal Marine orderlies prepared meals in the Mess. There was a very simple menu: cold meat, soup, bacon and eggs, cheese and biscuits and other such simple fare. Jacob thought 'there was decent food there' but Jock Colville, who occasionally dined there and was more used to the food at his clubs, the Travellers and Whites, or restaurants like the Mirabelle, was rather more critical and quickly 'tired of tinned food and sausages'.[8]

The management, not just of the War Rooms but of the machinery of the higher command, was largely in the capable hands of the secretariat. That the machinery worked smoothly owed much to the good relations between Sir Edward Bridges and General Ismay. Bridges, head of the secretariat, has been well described by Joan Bright of the Cabinet Office:

> Sir Edward Bridges, son of a poet [his father was the Poet Laureate, Robert Bridges], with a poet's unruly hair, a man of shy charm, held his high post with such modesty that he managed to merge his considerable intellect into a balanced whole of unobtrusive leadership and tactful cooperation with colleagues trimmed for war. His relationship with General Ismay was one of mutual respect and forbearance between two widely different temperaments, and there was no shadow of disloyalty or intrigue between them. They were immune to the measles of over-staffing and kept the War Cabinet Offices compact and flexible, as expeditious as a well-oiled machine.[9]

Colville depicts Bridges rather differently: 'Friendly, apt to give one a playful punch in the tummy on meeting [not quite 'shy' charm!], he was a forceful and outspoken man with a high sense of public service and propriety.' He agrees, however, that Bridges and Ismay were the 'twin pillars on which the prime minister rested'.[10]

Bridges was the chief link between Churchill and the main civil and military departments of state, just as Ismay was the link with the chiefs of staff and their various committees. Martin Gilbert describes how, under Bridges, the War Cabinet Office became a 'sort of prime minister's department in which the secretary held together the civil and military branches', a process assisted by putting important military and civilian staff in the same office. The Treasury, which had traditionally exercised some of the functions taken over by Bridges, was kept at arm's length, due largely to the poor relations between its professional head, Sir Horace Wilson, and Churchill.[11] Although Churchill had a high opinion of Bridges and relied on his advice, he did not find him as convivial a companion as Ismay. Norman Brook, who became deputy secretary to the War Cabinet in 1942, was also more to his taste in this respect.[12] It was never enough with Churchill that a man should do his job efficiently and conscientiously: his affection and regard were won by the establishment of personal empathy, never an easy genie to conjure up.

Lieutenant-General Jacob described the military section of the secretariat as 'A small, very closely-knit and informal office, with no protocol and all that sort of nonsense and, I think, highly efficient'. The threesome who ran it worked together harmoniously. Pug Ismay has already been described and it was he, above all, who, with his personal charm, intelligence and administrative ability, gave the secretariat and the War Rooms their ethos. Leslie Hollis was also a man of notable social skills. Colville maintains that he was 'liked by all', and Ian Jacob, in the *Dictionary of National Biography* entry for his old friend, described him as 'full of common sense, completely loyal, and straight as a die'. He was informal in a rather starchy age, and his secretary, Olive Margerison, called him 'Jo' in private. Both Ismay and Hollis had a keen sense of the ridiculous. Olive Margerison tells of a time when she walked past Hollis's door during an air-raid and saw:

> ... all three chiefs of staff on the floor flat on their faces, with Brigadier Hollis under a desk. She was astounded when she heard him say, looking up at her: 'Why aren't you afraid? You're the bravest person I've met!' Olive's reply was: 'I'm not frightened, just foolhardy!' and Hollis and the chiefs crept out from their shelter. He laughed and said: 'Let's have a drink', and opened up the bottle of gin he kept tucked away in the cabinet for emergencies.[13]

Jacob was rather different and, though he was very much the professional soldier, is often termed 'donnish', in part due to his formidable intellect, but also because of his rather austere manner and appearance. He was nicknamed 'Iron Pants' by Brigadier Anthony Head,[14] who worked with the Joint Planners, and, perhaps because he concentrated wholly upon the job in hand, 'his clear brain felt no need for bothering too much about personal relationships in the office'.[15] He was certainly not without emotion. When, in August 1942, Churchill sacked Sir Claude

Auchinleck, CinC Middle East, Jacob handed him the fatal letter. It was, he recalled, like murdering an unsuspecting friend.

The apparatus for directing the war, over which Churchill presided, has been seen as an exemplar for war organisation, comparing favourably with those of other combatants and providing a model for America's Combined Chiefs of Staff as established in 1942.[16] Whether any organisation led by Churchill could be seen purely in terms of a management system may, however, very much be doubted. The machinery was in place, but Churchill's character made its operation idiosyncratic and very much dependent on the lifestyle, friendships, animosities and enthusiasms of the man in charge.

As we have seen, Churchill inherited much of this machinery from the careful planning of the CID: a War Cabinet, its secretariat and the Chiefs of Staff Committee. He added the Defence Committee (Operations), which channelled the recommendations of the chiefs of staff to the War Cabinet. Even the Defence Committee became less important over time, and running the war was left largely to Churchill and the chiefs of staff, with occasional staff conferences, which brought together ministers with particular interests, Churchill and the chiefs. The most important feature of this tight and effective organisation for waging war was the combination of civilian authority with military advice, and much of its effectiveness came from the centralisation of ultimate control in Whitehall, largely in the NPO.

The chiefs of staff

It is hard to overemphasise the importance of what went on in the NPO and its hardened basement, the CWR. If there was no re-run of the bitter guerrilla war between the 'frocks' and the 'brass hats', the politicians and the generals, that had disfigured British strategy during the First World War, neither was there constant amity. The prime minister's authority and leadership were recognised, but his interference, enthusiasms and initiatives were often resented. On the whole the result was a fruitful compromise, a synthesis between daring and caution, soaring amateurism and hardened professionalism, optimism and pessimism. However, differences between Churchill and the chiefs of staff were more serious than is often recognised. That they were usually reconciled (though occasionally with tantrums on the one side and anguish on the other) had much to do with the fact that the chiefs and the prime minister inhabited the same headquarters and saw each other almost every day, be it upstairs in the NPO or poring over the maps downstairs in the Map Room. The process also owed much to the efficient machinery of the War Cabinet secretariat and the emollient influences of Pug Ismay and Edward Bridges.

Despite Churchill's great authority, there were implicit checks and balances to his power over the chiefs of staff. To overrule the combined advice of the heads of the three services would have exposed the prime minister to the risk of losing the support in Parliament on which his position ultimately depended, and a chief of staff who was unalterably opposed to a decision had the right to put his disagreement in writing. With another prime minister things might have been very different but Churchill, when out-argued or presented with steadfast resistance, was usually prepared to give way to professional advice on strictly military matters. That consensus or compromise eventually prevailed, though often not without those essential commodities blood, toil, tears and sweat, was a triumph over the real differences that often existed.

Churchill's deep faith in his own destiny and that of his nation – the two not always easily distinguishable – gave him too much confidence in the strength of Britain's forces and stood in sharp contrast to his senior military advisers' rational recognition of the nation's frailty. They realised that the British army had been weakened by decades of neglect, and had considerable respect for the ability of the German army. Alan Brooke, for instance, was ever conscious that the First World War had winnowed the ranks of his able contemporaries and that the combination of years of reduced military expenditure and a national mindset which had devalued military virtues meant that the British army was far from the remarkable fighting force it had been in the summer of 1918.

Churchill wanted generals who were confident, aggressive and charismatic, who would push on and get results. Senior commanders were less convinced that these were necessarily the qualities that would guarantee success, and preferred careful preparation, the husbanding of men and materials, and dogged professionalism. Above all, they were horrified by Churchill's desire for action at all costs, his demand for raids on the French coast, his periodic obsession with landings in Norway and his eternal enthusiasm (mirroring his attitude in the First World War) for new fronts. General Brooke's diary entry for 11 November 1940 reads:

> PM was having chiefs of staff meeting to discuss Greek situation. Are we again going to have 'Salonika supporters' like the last war? Why will politicians never learn the simple principle of concentration of force at the vital point, and the avoidance of dispersal of effort?[17]

Having replaced General Sir Edmund Ironside with General Sir John Dill as CIGS, by the summer of 1941 Churchill had turned against Dill. He was dissatisfied with Wavell, blaming him for defeats in North Africa ('Wavell etc had been very silly in North Africa', he grumbled, 'and should have been prepared to meet an attack there') and for failing to construct adequate defences in Crete. He was actually asking Wavell to do too much with limited resources, and when he replaced him with General Sir Claude Auchinleck, the same pattern was repeated. He now rounded on Dill, who supported Auchinleck. Dill has been described as having a 'quick mind' allied to 'a quiet manner, concealing a strong will'.[18] But Churchill, often a man to judge by first impressions, was not in the least impressed by the quiet manner and replaced Dill with General Sir Alan Brooke, a gunner who was, like so many other great soldiers, of Ulster stock and whose almost donnish appearance veiled adamantine moral courage.

Brooke and Churchill had a stormy relationship but, ultimately, an effective one. The CIGS ('Brookie' to his master) rarely hesitated to stand up to the prime minister and managed to deflect him from some of his crazier schemes. Whether they actually loved each other, as one of Alanbrooke's best biographers has suggested,[19] is doubtful, for Brooke's exasperation with Churchill went deeper than the flashes of anger recorded in his diary, while Churchill did not treat Brooke well, failing to support him for the command of Operation 'Overlord' (though in fairness, while Overlord worked well enough without Brooke, he could not really be spared from the central direction of the war) and being less than effusive about his contribution to victory in his book, *The Second World War.* However, it is certain that there was mutual respect, and the soaring imagination and the systematic mind proved a highly effective combination. Well might historian Andrew Roberts point to the centrality of the Churchill-Brooke relationship in his *Masters and Commanders* (2008).

Churchill's relations with the admirals have been aptly described as 'always delicate'.[20] Well aware of his record of intervening in naval operations, they found his interference hard to bear. Churchill found Sir Andrew Cunningham, CinC Mediterranean Station for much of the war, too defensively minded and subjected him to what the admiral called 'ceaseless prodding'. There were important aspects of modern naval warfare he never fully grasped. He did not appreciate the methods of convoy protection, for he was never satisfied with the defensive and thought support vessels should be employed like cavalry skirmishers. No less important was his failure (shared, it must be said, by many naval officers) to understand that capital ships required air cover. The latter blind spot (upon which the events in Norway 1940 should surely have thrown some light) led to the loss of HMS *Prince of Wales* and HMS *Repulse* on 10 December 1941. Admiral of the Fleet Sir Dudley Pound managed to retain his confidence sufficiently to be kept on as a chief of staff long after his declining health should have ensured his retirement. He was suffering from a brain tumour and died in harness in 1943 but might well have retired earlier if he had not feared that Churchill would block the appointment of his obvious successor, Cunningham, who argued firmly that, though ships had to be risked to gain victory, the fleet must be kept in being or command of the sea could be lost.

On the whole Churchill's relations with his air marshals were more harmonious than those with his generals and admirals. As secretary of state for War and Air in 1919 he had supported the establishment of an independent air force and had been an early proponent of the concept that bombing could win wars. In his first year as prime minister bombing was the only way to get at the main enemy, and Bomber Command accordingly enjoyed his full support. Air Chief Marshal Sir Charles Portal was the most taciturn of the chiefs of staff, contributing to discussions only when he had to, and Churchill, who felt less confident in his knowledge of air warfare than he did about naval and military matters, rarely interfered with his plans, though there was an explosive outburst when, after the Soviet Union had entered the war, Portal disagreed with the prime minister's offer to send ten RAF squadrons to assist it. Churchill's faith in the effectiveness of Bomber Command and the damage it could do to Germany was, however, shaken by the Butt Report of 1941. Instigated by Lindemann, Churchill's scientific adviser, it exposed the fact that only about one third of bombers had actually reached the very general area of their target. However, Air Marshal Sir Arthur Harris, the single-minded head of Bomber Command, received support from Portal and Lindemann for a continuation of the bombing campaign using new technology and heavier bombers, but now applying area bombing which aimed to 'dehouse' German workers and smash war production. Churchill, with occasional reservations, supported what was later to become a controversial aspect of Britain's war.

The sort of commander Churchill admired was a man with a record of personal bravery and a zeal for striking at the enemy. Discretion and careful preparation involving the amassing of superior force did not rank high in comparison with dash and vigour. Admiral Sir Roger Keyes, who had commanded the daring raid on the U-boat bases at Ostend and Zeebrugge in 1918, possessed élan in copious quantities. An MP, he had played a prominent part in the debate which brought Chamberlain's government down and continuously demanded that Churchill give him a prominent role in the war. He was appointed to the new post of adviser on Combined Operations, but as he tended to offend and irritate he was replaced by Lord Louis Mountbatten, and the appointment was raised in 1942 to that of chief of Combined Operations. Mountbatten certainly had a dashing record, though it involved sunk and battered ships, and many naval officers thought him showy, pretentious and inclined to make too much of being a member of the royal family. Naval historian Richard Ollard maintains that 'Certainly there was nothing in his unfortunate record as a sea officer to justify so inexplicable an appointment.'[21] Only a captain on his appointment to Combined Operations, he was swiftly promoted to acting vice-admiral, given army and air force ranks as well, and became a member of COS Committee. He went on to exercise supreme command in the Far East, inducing Alan Brooke to write, on 7 August 1945: 'Seldom has a supreme commander been more deficient in the main attributes of a supreme commander than Dickie Mountbatten.'

Had Churchill enjoyed untrammelled authority over the chiefs, the result would have almost certainly been disastrous, with armies and ships endangered for the sake of action rather than in measured pursuit of strategic goals. In contrast, had things been left entirely to the chiefs, caution might have prevented many useful initiatives. In the end, the balance between energetic prosecution of the war and a realistic appraisal of strength was generally maintained. Above all, Churchill had the greater responsibilities and the wider vision. And taking the struggle as a whole, the strategy of even the best general was rightly limited to winning the war, but Churchill had to consider the diplomatic dimension and, as the conflict ground remorselessly on, the shape of the post-war world and Britain's position within it.

Churchill's court

If the theoretical structure of war direction may have been an exemplary management system, its practical operation was laced with both dynamism and eccentricity. Alongside, and intruding into the formal structures, committees and decision-making, was what may best be termed Churchill's court. This did not just include his private secretaries, his family and his favoured friends and advisers, for it drew into its charmed circle ministers, civil servants and senior officers. As at a mediaeval court, courtiers had to dance to the rhythm of the monarch's day: members of the inner circle found themselves summoned to the prime minister's bedroom to confront the great man working on his dispatch boxes, or stayed up into the small hours listening drowsily to his perorations.

His daily routine was unconventional. Whenever possible, he awoke about 8.30 and enjoyed a 'proper' breakfast, which often consisted of cold game, before spending much of the morning in bed, reading the morning papers and the documents in his dispatch boxes. He then took a bath; baths were very important to him and he usually had one in the late afternoon as well; the lack of baths down in the CWR was one reason why he never really warmed to the place. Fortified by a substantial lunch, taken invariably at 1.30 and accompanied by his favourite Pol Roger champagne, he would take a nap at some time before dinner. After dinner he put in several hours of work at meetings and talking informally to colleagues before, on many nights, dictating to secretaries until any time up to 4.30 in the morning. He hated being disturbed, had a special mat installed so that the hobnailed boots of the Marine sentry outside his quarters in No. 10 Annexe were silenced, and had a particular horror of the whistling so beloved of messengers and junior clerks.

Few men, it has been said, are a hero to their valet: but Churchill remained a hero not only to his valet, Frank Sawyers, but to a considerable number who saw him dressing and undressing, or draped only in a towel. Not perhaps since the levées of eighteenth-century monarchs have so many powerful men attended a leader in his boudoir or in various stages of déshabille. Ismay would spend mornings running through the business of the day while sitting beside his bed, and Brooke was often summoned to the bedroom to find Churchill lying in his red, green and gold dressing-gown, smoking a cigar. Once Churchill received him as soon as he came out of his bath:

> ... looking like a Roman Centurion with nothing on except a large bath towel draped around him! He shook me warmly by the hand in this get up and told me to sit down while he dressed. A most interesting procedure, first he stepped into a white silk vest, then white silk drawers, and walked up and down the room in this kit, looking rather like 'Humpty Dumpty' with a large body and small thin legs![22]

The No. 10 Annexe flat was also the entrance to the office of his staff, and visitors arriving early for appointments would occasionally 'be astonished to be confronted by a figure enveloped in an enormous white bath towel crossing back to the bedroom from the bathroom ... and the visitor would be put at his ease by a stately greeting from the towel-clad figure'.[23]

Churchill had acquired a number of confidants, who, during his 'wilderness years' out of office, had provided him with the sort of assistance that a minister usually receives from Whitehall officials. These 'familiars' were a talented and unorthodox, though not wholly reliable, group. As we have seen, Ismay had worried that this coterie might supersede the secretariat and, though most of its members were given formal appointments, they were certainly seen by established politicians, civil servants and senior officers as a threat to their authority, an alternative to normal channels of command and even as loose cannons sliding about the slippery decks of Whitehall. Foremost among them were Frederick Lindemann, Brendan Bracken and Desmond Morton, all of whom were allocated rooms in the CWR and in No. 10 Annexe. All three were bachelors, and as Geoffrey Best has suggested, were 'more likely than married men to give him [Churchill] their entire attention'.[24]

Frederick Lindemann, known to Churchill as 'the Prof', had been a member of Churchill's circle since the 1920s. He was Professor of Experimental Physics at Oxford, had studied in Germany and had inherited a fortune. Something of a polymath, he was highly intelligent and had strong views on almost everything. Ismay opined that: 'He seemed to have a poor opinion of the intellect of everyone with the exception of Lord Birkenhead, Mr Churchill and Professor Lindemann.'[25] As Lord Birkenhead (formerly F. E. Smith, the sharp-brained lawyer, bon viveur and friend of Churchill's political youth) was now dead, that left only Churchill and the Prof himself. Before the war he advised

Churchill on rearmament, and may well have been responsible for convincing him that bombing was the key to victory. When Churchill became first lord of the Admiralty in 1939, he had invited the Prof to join him, and Lindemann had set up 'S Branch' a statistical department, which he persuaded his Oxford colleague, Roy Harrod, a distinguished economist, to join. When he became prime minister, Churchill installed Lindemann as his personal assistant and in 1942 he became paymaster-general.

His overweening arrogance did not endear him to government scientific advisers or military experts, but Churchill trusted his advice completely. He was not always right, for he underestimated the ability of Germany to develop rocket weapons, and has been criticised for not backing the development of radar by the government's scientific adviser, Sir Henry Tizard, but he did alert Churchill to the importance of science in the 'wizard war'.

Lindemann was always immaculately dressed ('like a butler', said Roy Jenkins), drove a Hispano-Suiza car and was a tremendous snob. A vegetarian and almost a teetotaller, he was an unlikely boon companion for Churchill, but his advice on scientific matters and the statistical information he collected were found invaluable. Unsurprisingly, Lindemann made many enemies, among them Lord Beaverbrook and Churchill's son-in-law Duncan Sandys, and he returned animosity implacably: he was no better loved in Whitehall than he had been at Oxford. Colville observed acidly, when Lindemann was about to be ennobled in June 1941, that it 'will cause anger in many quarters and especially at Oxford, but not as much as when it is learned that he proposes to call himself Lord Cherwell of Oxford'.[26] Lindemann did, however, do much to ensure that the armed forces developed weaponry based on scientific innovations, and his Statistical Section provided an effective audit of the efficiency of armaments production and the damage done by Bomber Command. Lindemann, like Churchill, also favoured and protected unconventional men, who, scorned or ignored by superiors, had a contribution to make. These were folk like the engineer officer Millis Jefferis, who invented the limpet mine and the 'sticky bomb', which stuck to its target, and Major-General Percy Hobart, who developed the specialist armoured vehicles, known as the 'Funnies' for use in the Normandy landings where they made an invaluable contribution in enabling the British to break through beach obstacles.

Brendan Bracken was an oddity, who would have been hard to believe in a work of fiction. Born in Ireland, he had spent his adolescence in Australia before reinventing himself in his early twenties by pretending to be younger than he was, and persuading the headmaster of Sedbergh School to admit him to the sixth form. Boldly presenting himself to Churchill, he won his place as a disciple and adviser. By the 1930s, he had become MP for South Paddington and a successful publisher of journals, including what became the *Financial Times.* With his unruly red hair, thick glasses and poor teeth, he was not prepossessing in appearance but he had great charm, keen intelligence and an encyclopaedic memory. He became Churchill's parliamentary private secretary in 1940 and was then, rather against his will, persuaded to become Minister of Information in 1941, a post in which Sir John Reith and Duff Cooper had been unsuccessful but in which Bracken excelled and held for the rest of the war. Even after he became a minister, he continued to spend evenings at No. 10 Annexe and to be a regular companion to Churchill. He was a consummate storyteller, though many of his recollections owed more to his imagination than to his experiences. Nobody was better able to cajole Churchill out of a bad mood than Bracken. Most people ended up liking him and, indeed, a pre-war Minister of Agriculture raised laughter in the House of Commons when he quipped that there was 'no known method of suppressing Bracken'.

Major Sir Desmond Morton (knighted in 1945) was one of the few men to have survived being shot through the heart. Having recovered from his wound, incurred while serving in France in the First World War, he became ADC to Field Marshal Haig. In 1934, he was appointed director of the Industrial Intelligence Centre, a rather misleadingly named organisation which was attached to the CID, its purpose to glean information about German rearmament. He lived close to Churchill's house, Chartwell, in Kent, and passed on much of this information, clearly in contravention of the Official Secrets Act. Whether, as Churchill later claimed, this was done with the permission of the prime ministers of the 1930s is, to say the least, unclear. Perhaps Ramsay Macdonald, Stanley Baldwin and Neville Chamberlain pursued a complex strategy in seeking negotiated settlements to Germany's grievances, while at the same time allowing Churchill the information he needed so that Parliament and the public could be alerted to the need for rearmament in case such negotiations failed. Certainly, the extent to which Churchill was able to back up his claims about Germany's armaments programme with facts owed much to Morton. In May 1940 he was given a rather undefined role as an adviser to Churchill on intelligence matters. He was considered by some in 1940 and 1941 to be the most influential of the prime minister's inner circle. Henry 'Chips' Channon, certainly no friend of Churchill and his coterie, wrote:

> At his [Churchill's] almost Papal court, the new Cardinal, Morton, is an Oppenheim character. His rival, Professor Lindemann, the Berlin-born scientist and snob, remains, to his chagrin, no more than Bishop-in-Partibus but yearns for a Biretta. Roy Harrod, a theoretical oriental looking don, is the Monsignore of the Churchillian conclave. [27]

Partly because he talked up his influence with Churchill and partly because he was associated with secret intelligence, a subject which exercises enduring fascination, Morton's role may have been exaggerated. He was, nevertheless, useful to Churchill in maintaining relations between the prime minister's office and the Foreign Office, the Secret Service and governments in exile, particularly Charles de Gaulle's Free French.

Both intelligence and deception (the deliberate misleading of the enemy) were very important facets of the Second World War. Although Churchill was responsible for setting up the Special Operations Executive, with the wonderful job description, 'Set Europe Ablaze', Jock Colville, who was in a position to know, thought that his interest waned once it had been created. 'The Special Operations executive and other clandestine organisations, however effective, did not attract his attention', he affirmed. Nor did resistance movements in Europe, with the exception of the Titoist partisans in Yugoslavia, with whom his son Randolph was involved, really attract him.[28] He was, however, very interested in the sort of intelligence that could be learned from listening to the enemy's communications. The Joint Intelligence Committee, set up in 1936, was responsible for collating and assessing military intelligence. The fact that it embodied faults, largely emanating from interservice and interdepartmental rivalries, that stood in the way of a comprehensive assessment of information was demonstrated by the failure to correctly predict German intentions in Norway and France in the spring of 1940. Sir Harry Hinsley, the historian of British Intelligence, has commented that the JIC was 'still only moderately efficient – before the summer of 1941' and that, but for Churchill's personal interest, 'the development of an effective system for coordinating the assessment of intelligence and giving general direction to its use would have taken even longer than it did'.[29] It was, though, fortunate that Churchill became prime minister just as the first real breakthrough in the decoding of messages scrambled in the German 'Enigma' machine was taking place at the Government Communications HQ at Bletchley Park.

The establishment at Bletchley Park of a team of brilliant, often eccentric, individuals with a variety of academic backgrounds is an example of the far from invariable ability of Britain to harness the right expertise in the interests of the war effort. The significance of the material (at first called 'Boniface' but soon known as 'Ultra', the code name used by the Air

Ministry and Admiralty) was imparted to Churchill by Desmond Morton and Brigadier Stewart Menzies, 'C', the head of the Secret Intelligence Service. Having been alerted to what he called this 'goose that laid golden eggs', Churchill, impatient with the way the JIC appeared to sift the material too laboriously, insisted upon being sent the decrypted reports himself. His fascination with original material may have stemmed from his experience at the Admiralty in the first months of the First World War, and with his multi-volume work on his illustrious ancestor 'Duke John', the 1st Duke of Marlborough, who owed much of his success to the collation of intelligence gathered across the whole of Europe. The Ultra decrypts came to Churchill in faded yellow boxes stamped VRI (Victoria Regina Imperatrix). So well was the secret kept from all but a select few that even Ismay's personal assistant thought that 'Boniface' was the name of a spy planted in the German General Staff.[30]

Churchill's addiction to Ultra intelligence was a mixed blessing. His intercepts arrived rapidly but raw, and he sometimes jumped to conclusions. This added to tensions between him and the chiefs of staff, who preferred to await more measured digests from the JIC. By the summer of 1941 there were so many decrypts that even Churchill had to be content with mainly receiving summaries, while a combination of the sheer amount of Ultra material and the chiefs' annoyance at finding the prime minister ahead of them on some issues led to increased staffing of the JIC and a consequent acceleration in the production of its reports. Churchill's recognition of the importance of Ultra did much to create the enlarged team of experts that laboured in the CWR discussing, analysing and condensing the torrent of information that Bletchley Park released.

Churchill also brought into his inner circle and the War Cabinet his old colleague Lord Beaverbrook. The Canadian-born press baron, who had been Minister of Information at the end of the First World War, had, at different times, been both a friend and an opponent of Churchill's. A tempestuous and unpredictable figure, his appointment in May 1940 as Minister of Aircraft Production was not universally welcomed. Beaverbrook was not a team player, and his disregard for labour relations led to rows with Ernest Bevin, Minister for Labour, while he quarrelled with the Air Ministry, which was horrified by his demands for what would have been virtually a private military force for the protection of aircraft factories. Nevertheless, he got things done and made a major contribution to the Battle of Britain, for his draconian actions boosted aircraft production and by mid-August 1940 the total of Spitfires and Hurricanes available to Fighter Command had risen from the 331 after Dunkirk to 620.[31] That August he became a member of the War Cabinet.

A list of those who would have accompanied Churchill to Spetchley House, if the plans for the Black Move had ever been implemented, is revealing. Rooms had been prepared there for Churchill and his wife, their daughter Mary, for Sawyers, the valet, and for Mrs Landemare, the cook, as well as for six others: Desmond Morton, Eric Seal, Anthony Bevir (who dealt with patronage matters), Kathleen Hill, senior shorthand-typist, Professor Lindemann and his valet, Mr Harvey. The list sums up the half-private, half-public nature of Churchill's ménage.

Churchill's movements were unpredictable and plans were often changed at short notice, with fresh arrangements having to be made for the prime minister and his considerable entourage and baggage. These were the province of Commander Charles Thompson, who had been Churchill's flag lieutenant at the Admiralty. He accompanied Churchill on all his travels, looking somewhat simian, and was, according to Colville, treated 'rather like a slightly spoilt spaniel'.[32] Almost always in the background was another Thompson, Churchill's bodyguard, Detective Sergeant Walter Thompson, later promoted to inspector, who had protected Churchill in the early 1920s, when he had been negotiating with the IRA, and who served him for many years. He had early established his relationship to the man he protected when, after Churchill had wandered off on his own, he complained:

> 'Look, sir, we can't have this. How can I possibly look after you if you treat me like this? You're making my job quite impossible.'
>
> 'In future I will do all I can to help you Thompson. We've just begun to understand each other.'[33]

On his retirement, he had opened a grocery store, but in 1939 Churchill, having been warned of assassination threats, sent him a telegram, 'Meet me at Croydon Airport 4.30 p.m. Wed. Churchill', and employed him as a private protector. When war broke out, Thompson rejoined the police and became Churchill's bodyguard for the duration of the conflict. Looking after the prime minister was never an easy task. Once, in 1940, Churchill had promised his wife, Clementine, that he would go to bed in his bedroom in the underground War Rooms but, having clambered into bed, he summoned the detective. 'Well Thompson, pick up my clothes', he said. 'I kept my promise to Mrs Churchill. I came downstairs to bed, but I am now going upstairs to sleep.'[34] The prime minister's 'total disregard for danger when he walked the streets when bombs were falling' or roamed St James's Park in the dark with a torch attached to his walking stick by a special leather fitting, made him a difficult charge. On one occasion he was very nearly seriously injured when, as he was talking to Sir John Anderson at the entrance to the Annexe, an anti-aircraft shell hit the railings opposite and exploded, with a fragment wounding another bodyguard, Detective Sergeant Cyril Davies, who was standing close to him, in the thigh. Given that Davies was taller than his charge, Churchill would have been hit in the stomach if the fragment had struck him.[35]

Family, personal staff, private secretaries, the secretariat, ministers and senior officers lived interwoven lives. Churchill's wife and youngest daughter, Mary, lived with him in No. 10 Annexe, with Mary often sleeping in the bedroom reserved for Mrs Churchill in the CWR. Jack Churchill, his younger brother, lived at either No. 10 or the Annexe, while his older children, Randolph, Diana and Sarah, were frequent visitors to the Annexe and to Chequers when their duties, for all were in the services, allowed. Randolph, gifted, but spoiled and arrogant, was unpopular with most of the rest of the court; he had an adventurous war, first becoming an officer in his father's old regiment, the 4th Hussars, then volunteering for the Commandos and then the SAS and ending up with Tito – and the novelist Evelyn Waugh – in Yugoslavia,[36] having been elected MP for Preston along the way. Diana was a WRNS officer until she resigned her commission in 1940 after her husband, Duncan Sandys, was badly injured in a motor accident. Sarah, her marriage to the comedian Vic Oliver having broken down, was in the WAAF and Mary, the youngest, joined the ATS. The private secretaries, and to a lesser degree the secretariat and even the chiefs of staff, found their official responsibilities merging with the life of the Churchill family as they attended on the prime minister.

The Churchills were close but not always harmonious. Clementine Churchill was a devoted if in some ways a difficult wife, but Churchill could be an extraordinarily difficult husband. A lifelong Liberal, she had rather disapproved of her husband's journey back to the Conservative Party and, brought up by her somewhat bohemian mother, whose marriage to her ostensible father had been brief, she had experienced little financial security in her youth and was perennially (and with good reason) fearful of her husband's extravagance. Churchill, who was 'easily satisfied by the best of everything', had bought a country house, Chartwell, that he could ill afford and had lost a considerable sum after the Wall Street crash. Clemmie had strong likes and dislikes; most of Churchill's close advisers came into the later category. Lindemann was an exception, but Bracken, perhaps because of the persistent though groundless rumours (which Bracken naughtily did nothing to dispel) that he was the prime minister's illegitimate son, was a bête noire for many years. She also hated Beaverbrook. Her relations with her son Randolph and eldest daughter, Diana, were stormy and, though she could be cordial with the private secretaries, any imagined slight or presumption could draw a frosty reprimand. Her fierce loyalty to her husband saw her order General Montgomery out of the house when he characteristically observed that all politicians were dishonest.[37]

Churchill worked those who served him, whether in No. 10, the War Rooms or at Chequers, and be they generals or typists, very hard indeed. He could see no reason why a man or woman engaged in anything quite so important and interesting as a war should want to take leave, spend an evening at home or even go to bed early. When Ismay, who had snatched only about three hours sleep the previous night, asked Churchill, who was in full flow, whether he could be excused because he needed to get a good night's sleep, Churchill said: 'Well, if you don't care who wins the war, go ahead.' Brooke was never to be bullied, still less when, in mid-September 1942, he was away grouse shooting, enjoying his only holiday of the year. Churchill telephoned, accusing him of being 'out of touch with the strategic situation' because he had not seen a telegram from General Alexander postponing an attack on Rommel. Brooke replied: 'I have not yet solved how I am to remain in touch with the strategic situation whilst in a grouse butt.' To the supplementary question of whether he had a cypher officer with him, he retorted, 'No, I do not take a cypher officer to load for me when I go grouse shooting.'[38]

When the long-suffering Clementine disagreed with her husband, she often wrote, instead of telling him to his face. She penned him a much-quoted letter in the first weeks of his premiership warning that he was being inconsiderate: 'there is a danger of your being generally disliked by your colleagues and subordinates because of your rough, sarcastic and overbearing manner.' In fact most of those who worked for him were aware of the great responsibilities he shouldered, were willing to work long hours and accepted the sudden explosions and harsh comments when things went wrong with no ill-feeling, though they would not have been human if they were not sometimes exasperated.

A new secretary needed strong nerves, not least because Churchill hated changes in his staff. Elizabeth Nel recounted her fear of making mistakes in the first weeks she worked for him. He insisted on typing being double-spaced, and on the first occasion she had to take dictation from him she sat down before the special noiseless typewriter and forgot to check that it was set to double-spacing. 'It was not long before, passing behind the typewriter he noticed the single spacing', she wrote. 'At once he went off like a rocket. I was a fool, a mug, an idiot: I was to leave his presence and one of the others was to appear.'[39] She reflected on another incident, when he looked dismayed to find that, still very new to the job, she had been detailed to go to Chartwell with him: 'He did not mean to be unkind. He was just heart and soul engaged in winning the war.'[40]

For several of those working in No. 10 Annexe and the CWR, Chequers became a further weekend annexe. Churchill made more use of the official prime ministerial country house than any other prime minister and very rarely went to his own house, Chartwell (a few minutes flying time from the south coast), during the war. Not unnaturally he enjoyed getting away from Whitehall for weekends and often set off on a

Thursday, but he took his work with him, his dispatch boxes, a private secretary and a typist and shorthand secretary, and there would be guests, perhaps for the whole weekend, for a single night or for lunch or dinner. These would usually include members of the secretariat, generals, admirals or air marshals, ministers and one or two of his close advisers. Ismay was regularly there, as was Lindemann, though he always slipped home to Oxford to sleep. Bracken, however, rarely went to Chequers, and was secretive as to where he spent his weekends. Among the private secretaries, Colville was most frequently in attendance before he persuaded Churchill to allow him to join the RAF. His mother, Lady Cynthia Colville, was a lady-in-waiting to Queen Mary, so he had at least second-hand knowledge of life at court and the protocols of dealing with a demanding superior.

Chequers was also the stage for cementing warm relations with the USA. Averell Harriman, Roosevelt's personal envoy, Harry Hopkins, his unofficial emissary, and Ambassador John G. Winant, who had succeeded the rather anti-British Joseph Kennedy, were frequent guests; one result of their long weekends at Chequers was increased Anglo-American understanding. Another, less predictable, was that Winant appears to have fallen, as Roy Jenkins put it, 'rather ethereally' in love with Sarah Churchill, while Harriman fell for Randolph Churchill's wife, Pamela.[41]

These weekends gave great opportunities for relaxation; walks in the Chilterns, tennis, which Clementine loved and at which Lindemann excelled, and that sadistic but apparently genteel game, croquet. The food and drink were always plentiful and of high quality, for Churchill did not believe in the 'spam on a gold plate' conspicuous austerity of the royal family. A part of each evening would be taken up by viewing a film, always chosen by Churchill – a favourite was *Lady Hamilton*, which Churchill demanded time and again, always weeping when Nelson died. At Chequers, the main focus, at meals and after the film, would always be the war. Churchill, by this time in his ornate dressing-gown, glass in hand and cigar lit and relit, would ruminate on developments and possible ventures, digress on historical parallels and weave complex tapestries of the future. Edith Watson described these early morning sessions as 'Winston's midnight follies'. Most guests would be inspired, but some, like Brooke, would be yearning for bed and wishing they were in their own homes. For Churchill there was no clear division between work and leisure. 'Of course I work wherever I am and however I am', he affirmed. 'That is what does me good.'[42]

Churchill's bohemian way of running the war would be given poor marks by any managerial handbook, which may point to the deficiencies of management theory, for it was actually highly effective. He exercised his authority as much by his informal contacts with his staff at Chequers or late at night in the No. 10 Annexe as in formal committees. And across the board there was never any doubt, any doubt at all, as to who was in charge.

A wider war

Back in the underground Map Room, manned twenty-four hours a day by the JPS, new arrows and fresh symbols speckled the walls as Germany launched its attack on the Soviet Union in June 1941. Operation 'Barbarossa' took Stalin by surprise but it certainly should not have done. Churchill, having hard information gleaned from Ultra, had sent him a warning, though he could not reveal his sources, and Stalin had warnings from his own intelligence services and the Soviet spy in Tokyo, Richard Sorge. Intelligence information is rarely believed unless it seems to confirm existing convictions, and Stalin refused to acknowledge the possibility that Hitler would attack him. In his research for *Absolute War* (2007) Christopher Bellamy discovered a Stalinesque scrawl across a memorandum affirming that invasion was imminent, affirming that the information was simply a 'provocation'. The fate of those who crossed Stalin was too well known for any official to risk crossing him twice, however persuasive the intelligence. Neither Hitler nor Stalin could tolerate the loyal opposition furnished by the likes of Brooke, and the loss was unquestionably theirs.

In principle Germany's attack upon Russia should have faced Britain with a moral dilemma. Britain had ostensibly gone to war with Germany to protect the integrity of Poland, and the Soviet Union had joined Germany in destroying it. Information emerging from Russia was comparatively limited, and there were still many in Britain who believed that the Soviet Union was indeed, in a phrase widely used at the time, a workers' paradise. Churchill took the pragmatic line that, if Germany attacked the devil, he would be on the devil's side, though it proved necessary to play down growing evidence of the Russian regime's devilish nature, even to the extent of pretending to believe that the Soviet Union was not responsible for the murder of thousands of Polish officers, many of whose bodies were discovered in a mass grave in Katyn Forest in 1943. Britain had at last found a continental sword, even if it was not expected to be a very sharp one, for few expected Soviet forces to put up much of a fight. But the maxim that Russia is never as weak, or as strong, as she appears was to prove true, and Churchill was determined to give her sufficient aid to keep her in the war. For the moment this was limited to sending weapons and supplies round the North Cape to Murmansk and Archangel. Some 14,000 merchant ships took part in the Arctic convoys, and 85 of them, with 16 of their Royal Navy escorts, were lost. Just as for years Anglo-American historians underestimated the impact of the Eastern Front upon the war as a whole, so Soviet historians downplayed the effect of western supplies in Russia's hour of greatest need.

This was the beginning of a less heroic, less innocent and more pragmatic war, a struggle in which Britain's power and her ability to control her own destiny would fade. The reactions of Guy Crouchback in Evelyn Waugh's trilogy *The Sword of Honour* stand as one response: shame that the war was no longer a clean fight against an evil, but rather a matter of taking sides between two evils. The recovery of the British Communist Party and the rise of its membership to some 60,000 was, together with a broader adulation of a 'glorious Soviet ally' and its bluffly patriarchal 'Uncle Joe', another. The reaction of the majority was, probably, rather like Churchill's, relief that Britain at last had an ally and that it should not be too particular about its character. But Churchill had a parallel agenda, the wooing of America.

Churchill was genuinely fond of the USA and, when called upon to address a joint meeting of Congress in 1941, speculated, not wholly frivolously, that had his ancestry been only slightly different (an American father and an English mother, instead of vice versa), he might have been there on his own account. A great believer in the power of his personality and of personal relations between leaders, he thought that he could charm and persuade the US president. When he had re-entered the government as first lord of the Admiralty in 1939, Churchill received a polite note from Roosevelt, who mentioned that they had met at an official dinner in Gray's Inn in 1918, when he himself had been assistant secretary of the Navy, and suggested that they keep in contact. Churchill later admitted that he had forgotten the occasion, but a correspondence began, with Churchill signing himself, 'Former Naval Person', and their letters became much more frequent after he became prime minister.

There is no doubt that Churchill overestimated both the closeness of his relationship with Roosevelt and the congruence of British and American interests. On the other hand, the United States had good reasons to fear the consequences if Britain was defeated and the Royal Navy destroyed and, for its own reasons, the Roosevelt administration was moving to a position of support for Britain short of actually entering the war. In September 1940 agreement was reached on the lease of bases in the West Indies and Newfoundland to the Americans in return for fifty rather out-of-date destroyers. If the USA got more from this deal than the British, it was at least a start of greater cooperation, and after the presidential election of November 1940 Roosevelt no longer needed to worry quite so much about opposition to closer ties with the British, even if he still had to tread carefully with Congress. In December Churchill sent Roosevelt a long letter itemising the supplies needed to maintain Britain's war effort, and in March 1941 'Lend-Lease', proposed by the president, was passed by Congress. It proved a lifeline for Britain, albeit an expensive one in the long run, and by 1942–43 about one-quarter of all Britain's munitions came through Lend-Lease. Indeed, Hitler cited Lend-Lease as one of his reasons for declaring war on America in December 1941.

America's official and unofficial representatives in Britain, Ambassador John G. Winant, Averell Harriman and Harry Hopkins, were all sympathetic to Britain's position and admirers of Churchill, while US journalists and broadcasters, led by Ed Murrow, sent back to America positive accounts of Britain's determination to resist. Nevertheless, US opinion polls still showed that a large majority of Americans were determined that US troops should not go 'over there' again, and Congress seemed similarly set against involvement in a European war.

It was against this background that Churchill and Roosevelt arranged to meet. The conference was kept a close secret, with Roosevelt going on a 'fishing trip' to Maine and then boarding a US cruiser in order to get to the rendezvous, Placentia Bay, Newfoundland. The British contingent set off in Churchill's special train – in effect a mobile hotel, office and communications centre, from Marylebone Station. It stopped to pick up the prime minister (in his 'grey-blue rompers') at Wendover, steamed on to Thurso, where the passengers embarked for Scapa Flow to board the battleship HMS *Prince of Wales.* The entourage consisted of: General Dill, Admiral Pound, Air Chief Marshal Sir Wilfred Freeman, Lindemann, Hollis, Jacob, John Martin (Churchill's principal private secretary), Brigadier 'Dumbie' Dykes (director of plans at the War Office) and Sir Alexander Cadogan (permanent under-secretary at the Foreign Office) along with the prime minister's personal staff (his valet, detective and naval aide) and two writers, Howard Spring and H.V. Morton, whom Brendan Bracken as minister of information had selected to observe the historic meeting. Harry Hopkins joined the party at Scapa Flow. It was a retinue that 'Cardinal Wolsey might have envied', commented Jock Colville.

The voyage to Newfoundland was uneventful despite stormy seas. Alexander Cadogan's sardonic diary records fine meals, 'a tub of admirable caviare given him [Churchill] by Joe Stalin ... with a good young grouse', with Churchill losing money at backgammon to Harry Hopkins, and films chosen by the prime minister, most of which did not appeal to Cadogan's more intellectual tastes.[43]

When they arrived at Placentia Bay, the prime minister and entourage, now joined by Lord Beaverbrook, who had flown across the Atlantic, went aboard the heavy cruiser USS *Augusta.* Churchill and Roosevelt retired for a tête-a-tête lunch and the rest enjoyed what Hollis called 'an excellent fork lunch'[44] and Alexander Cadogan, in contrast, thought 'a very unsatisfactory, dry, dejeuner à la fourchette'.[45] Churchill's reaction to the rule against alcohol on US warships is, perhaps fortunately, not recorded.

The meeting certainly generated some good will, but rather less than Churchill had hoped for. The most important practical outcome was that the USA took over responsibility for protecting shipping in the America–Iceland stretch of the Atlantic, but otherwise all that emerged was the Atlantic Charter, a joint declaration of principles, a document so vague that even Stalin was able to sign up to it at a later date. Churchill made the best he could of the outcome, and a film was released of highlights of the meeting including the Sunday morning service on the deck of the *Prince of Wales* at which both delegations, the ship's company and 250 US seamen and marines sang 'Onward Christian Soldiers' and 'O God, Our Help in Ages Past'.[46]

By the beginning of the winter of 1941–42, Britain was thus receiving valuable assistance from the USA, but Roosevelt seemed no nearer to entering the war. Churchill, in the words of Andrew Roberts, was reduced, like Dickens's Mr Micawber, to 'waiting for something to turn up'.[47] What turned up was the Japanese attack upon Pearl Harbor on 7 December and with it the beginning of the war in the Pacific. Even this might possibly not have brought the USA into the European war had not Germany and Italy declared war upon America four days later. There was now, at long last, a 'Grand Alliance' as formidable as that which Duke John had used to thwart the ambitions of Louis XIV. Churchill was back in his element, and the staff in the Map Room were busier than ever.

1. Winston Churchill and Captain Richard Pim in Churchill's personal map room in No. 10 Annexe. Pim, who kept this map room up-to-date, accompanied the prime minister on his travels abroad and set up a temporary map room wherever Churchill was.

2. A meeting of the Chief of Staff Committee in 1945. *Left to right*: Major-General Hollis (Secretary); Admiral of the Fleet Sir Andrew Cunningham; Field Marshal Sir Alan Brooke (Chairman); Marshal of the Royal Air Force Sir Charles Portal; General Sir Hastings Ismay; Colonel C. R. Price (Assistant Secretary).

3. Major-General Hollis and Lawrence Burgis in the Map Room within the Cabinet War Rooms. Manned night and day the Map Room was the heart of the command centre.

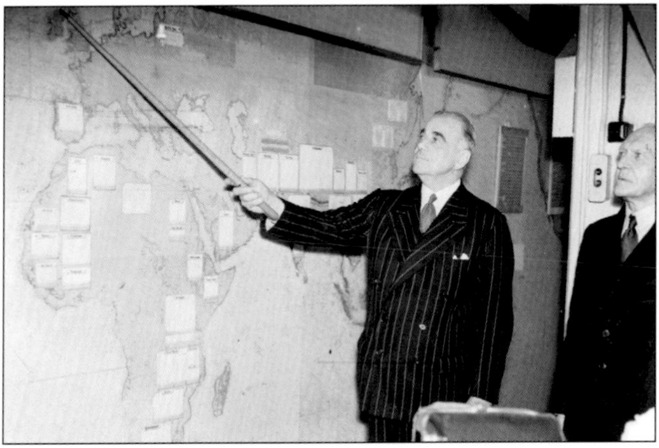

4. General Sir Hastings Ismay in the Map Room with Mr George Rance. Ismay's invaluable contributions to the command of Britain's war machine lay in his ability to smooth ruffled feathers and reconcile differences.

5. General Sir Alan Brooke in 1942. Professional, cautious and usually right, this determined Ulsterman complemented Churchill's more adventurous approach to the war.

6. The dining room in No. 10 Annexe, the suite of rooms on the ground and first floor of the New Public Offices to which the prime minister moved when 10 Downing Street was considered too vulnerable.

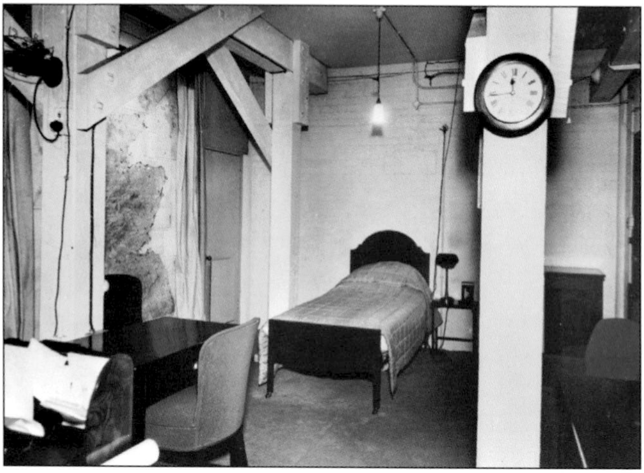

7. The Prime Minister's combined office and bedroom off the main corridor in the Cabinet War Rooms. Churchill, who disliked being underground, made almost no use of it.

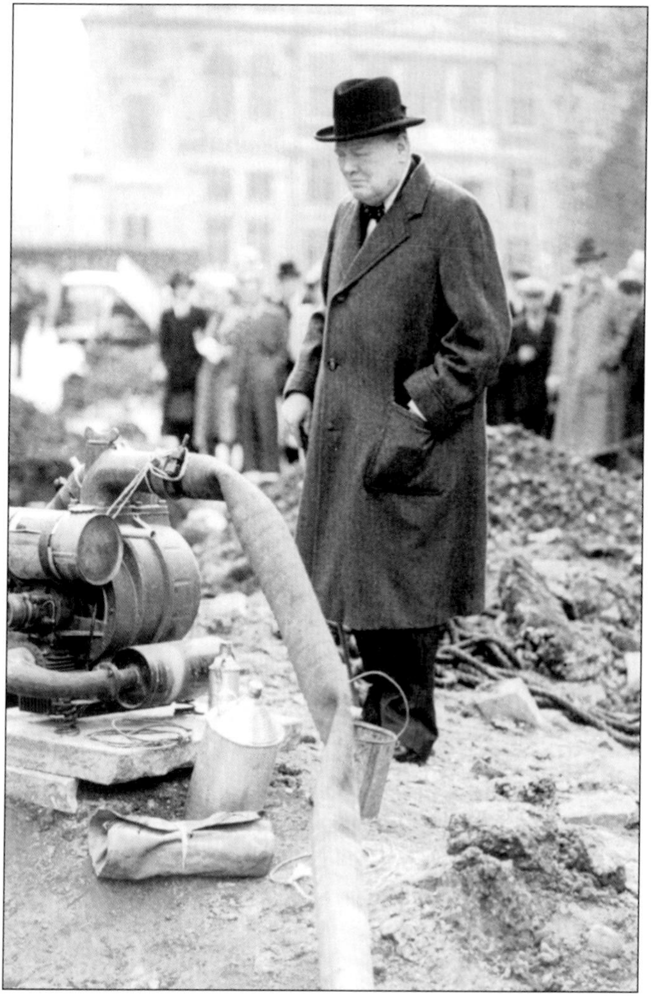

8. Churchill inspects the damage caused by a bomb that fell close to the Clive Steps at the north-west corner of the New Public Offices.

9. Preparations for a possible attack by German paratroops. A sandbag pillbox is constructed at the junction of Birdcage Walk and Great George Street.

LOW
ALL BEHIND YOU, WINSTON

10. Low's cartoon of 14 May 1940 was published in the *Evening Standard*. It depicts the nation rolling up its sleeves as it unites behind Churchill and the new government.

11. A view (circa 1980) of the Government Offices, Great George Street and New Public Offices. The photograph shows the western side of the building facing St James Park. The Cabinet War Rooms and No. 10 Annexe are on the left of the building.

12. The concrete apron wall that was built in front of the Cabinet War Rooms in 1940. It covered the area directly above the point where the protection provided by the 'Slab' ended.

13. Telephones, except for those fitted with scrambling devices, were not secure and conversations could be tapped into. This phone carries the message that 'Speech on telephones is not secure'. This was something that Churchill himself sometimes forgot.

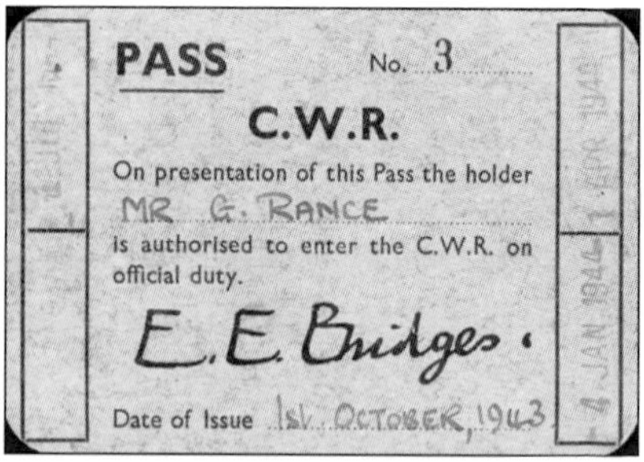

PASS No. 3

C.W.R.

On presentation of this Pass the holder MR G. RANCE is authorised to enter the C.W.R. on official duty.

E. E. Bridges.

Date of Issue 1st OCTOBER, 1943

14. Security required that everyone, even those who came in and out of the War Rooms on a daily basis, had to carry a pass like this one issued to George Rance.

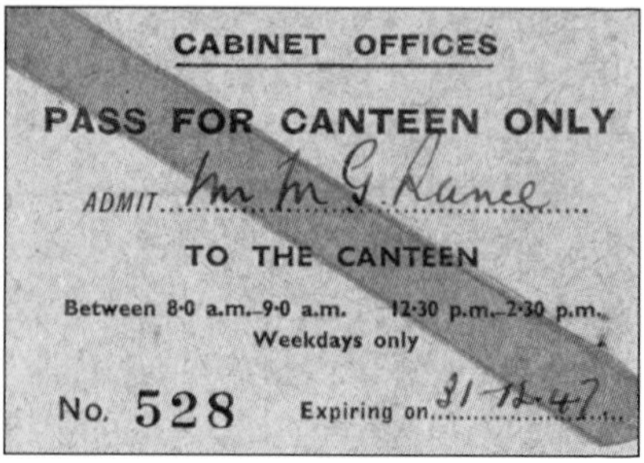

CABINET OFFICES

PASS FOR CANTEEN ONLY

ADMIT Mr G. Rance

TO THE CANTEEN

Between 8·0 a.m.–9·0 a.m. 12·30 p.m.–2·30 p.m.

Weekdays only

No. 528 Expiring on 31-12-47

15. He needed a separate pass to enter the canteen.

16. An efficient telephone system was crucial to the working of the Cabinet War Rooms as the switchboard had to be expanded several times. Eventually there was a combined No. 10 and War Cabinet office exchange located in the original corridor of the War Rooms.

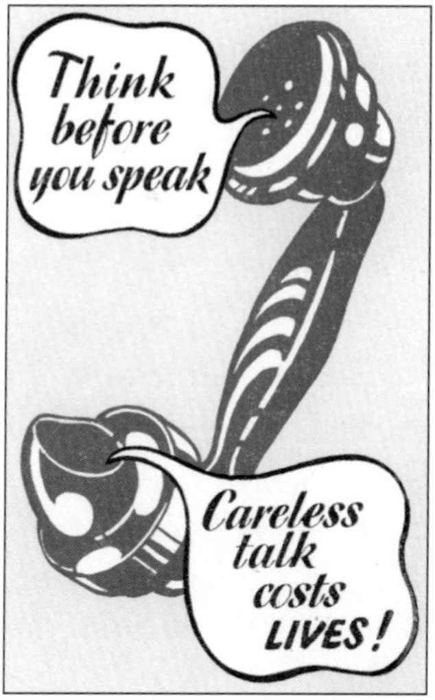

17. Numerous 'Careless Talk Costs Lives' posters were produced during the war. This one warns against indiscreet telephone calls.

18. The sub-basement, or the 'Dock', was a pretty grim area. It was furbished basically and there were rats. Yet, it was here that many of the staff of the War Rooms slept or tried to, as the lights were on constantly and there was the hum of the ventilating machinery.

19. Mr George Rance of the Office of Works operated a board indicating what the weather was like, for otherwise the staff in their underground world would not have known. He would insert the 'windy' board when there was a heavy air-raid.

20. A Heinkel He 111 bomber over London on 7 September 1940.

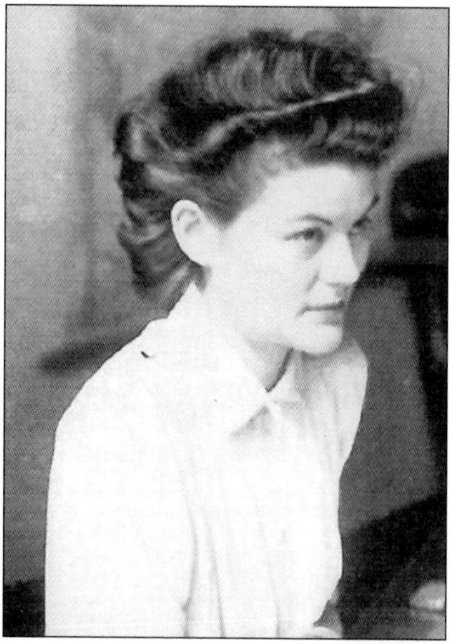

21. Joan Bright (later Joan Bright Astley) sitting in the information centre she set up to enable commanders-in-chief to keep abreast of events in all sectors of the war.

22. Ilene Hutchinson (later Ilene Adams). A stenographer, Ilene joined the War Cabinet Secretariat on the day war was declared. She worked first in Richmond Terrace and then at Storey's Gate, and went to Yalta with the British delegation.

23. Major-General Hollis and three of the secretaries from the War Cabinet Office at the Potsdam conference 1945. *From left to right*: Miss Olive Christopher; Miss Margaret Sutherland and Miss M. Gray. The remarkable group of women, who served in the War Cabinet Secretariat and in the War Rooms provided an efficient support to the British delegations for the war-time conferences.

24. The 'Big Three', Stalin, Roosevelt and Churchill at the Teheran Conference, November–December 1943.

25. A number of the WAAF cypher officers under the command of Squadron Officer Joan Williams were flown out to Marrakesh to provide communications support when Churchill was convalescing there in late December 1943 and January 1944. Here three of them find some time for sight-seeing during a break from work. *Left*: Joan Llewellyn (neeé Williams). *Centre:* Jean Hale (neé Rose).

26. Stalin toasts Churchill on the occasion of the prime minister's sixty-ninth birthday which fell on 30 November 1943 during the Teheran Conference. Anthony Eden stands on the other side of Churchill.

27. The victorious Chiefs of Staff with the prime minister on the day before Victory in Europe was announced. Major-General Hollis and General Sir Hastings Ismay stand behind. *Left to right*: Marshall of the RAF Sir Charles Portal, Field Marshall Sir Alan Brooke, Winston Churchill and Admiral of the Fleet Sir Andrew Cunningham.

4

LIFE IN THE BUNKER

A striking characteristic of Second World War Britain was the ability of its people to keep secrets. Cabinets and government departments – indeed, the whole structure of state and society – were, even before the war, much less 'leaky' than their modern successors. The press, for its part, was more cautious than it is today: there was widespread recognition that this was indeed a war of national survival. If a few of those who knew secrets were occasionally garrulous and incautious, a combination of remarkable innate integrity, well-publicised warnings that 'Hitler is listening' and fear of the consequences of indiscretion ensured that most people knew that careless talk might indeed cost lives, and kept their mouths firmly shut. 'Be Like Dad, Keep Mum' was how the government's posters put it. Such was the code of secrecy that couples courted and married, finding out only later that they had been working in adjacent buildings or even, perhaps, in different corridors in the same building. The hugely important role of Bletchley Park and the cracking of the German 'Enigma' code is perhaps the most famous example of this discretion, for the existence of the top-level Ultra intelligence that it produced was not revealed to the public until the mid-1970s. Those engaged in confidential work were reluctant to talk about it until long after the war had become history: I have always found this patriotic reticence one of the most admirable qualities of this remarkable generation.

The CWR were, it has been said, a 'well kept secret' and the work that went on there was known only to those 'who needed to know'. Here was the Map Room, which charted the advances and retreats of armies, the locations of warships and the often painful progress of those convoys that kept the nation supplied. Here the planners worked on future operations and the intelligence staff pondered the enemy's strength and assessed his next moves. But in one sense the War Rooms were rather like the busy domestic downstairs of an Edwardian household, with upstairs the more glamorous world of No. 10 Annexe, where Churchill lived and worked and the Cabinet secretariat had its main offices. The whole of the NPO building, usually referred to by insiders as Storey's Gate or Great George Street,[1] constituted a war headquarters, containing departments crucial to the prosecution of the war, and secrecy was required throughout the whole of it, upstairs as well as downstairs. Yet this was not deep in a distant forest or hidden in a walled-off suburb: it was in the very heart of the capital, fittingly within sight of Buckingham Palace and the Houses of Parliament, with taxis trundling along Birdcage Walk.

Ilene Adams, a shorthand typist who worked for Bridges, Ismay, Hollis and the JPS, was told: 'As soon as you've finished a bit of work, forget it.'[2] Everyone was warned not to keep diaries, and letters were censored. Behind the advice was the implicit threat of sanctions if there were leaks. Even reading newspapers was discouraged and Olive Christopher (later Margerison) was told: 'Refrain from reading the press because it would be easy to confuse what you do in your work with what you read in the daily newspapers.'[3] Ilene Adams remembers two men she thought were detectives coming in to the War Rooms and taking away a girl who was in floods of tears: 'We were all very scared', she admitted.

In general, despite occasional loose talk in clubs, pubs or on pillows, work – even where one worked – was kept secret. Olive Christopher, personal assistant to General Hollis, recalled that the generals thought 'that the lower ranks were better at keeping secrets, whereas the senior ranks would go off to their clubs and "spill the beans" playing bridge!'[4] and Squadron Officer Joan Williams (later Lady Llewellyn), who was in charge of the Cabinet Office Cypher Office (COCO), was sometimes horrified by the indiscreet talk she overheard in fashionable hotels and restaurants.[5] Certainly when it came to the keeping of diaries, the upper echelons were by far the worst offenders against the rule forbidding it. Historians have good reason to be grateful, for without the diaries of Lord Alanbrooke, John Colville and others our knowledge of the Second World War would be much the poorer.

Churchill himself, predictably enough, was never one to obey rules and hoarded papers which should have remained in official hands. His six-volume, highly idiosyncratic, account of the war came out between 1948 and 1954 and embodied some material which ought to have been subject to the normal regulations applying to public records. Lawrence Burgis, in complete defiance of the rules, secreted verbatim accounts of War Cabinet meetings.[6]

For many the habit of discretion prevailed long after it had ceased to be necessary. Nora Colville (later Hunter) was a WAAF Cypher Officer, and her daughter recalls that it was only in the late 1980s that she felt it proper to discuss with her family the work she had done for the War Cabinet.[7] The diaries and recollections of ministers, civil servants and senior officers began to emerge in the 1950s: Hollis's *One Marine's Tale*, was published in 1956 and James Leasor's *War at the Top*, based on Hollis's experiences, in 1959, while Ismay's *Memoirs* came out in 1960. Joan Bright Astley's *The Inner Circle*, the most evocative and incisive account of life in the secretariat, was published as late as 1971. It was, however, only with the restoration of the CWR by the Imperial War Museum in the 1980s that a concerted effort was made to gather information from many of those who had worked there, research which still continues. A more complete picture, not just of the layout of the rooms and of their relationship to the other parts of the command centre but of the nature of the work and the conditions and atmosphere (as much physical as psychological) in which it was conducted, could now be assembled.

Many people who did not work for the Cabinet Office

or in the CWR must have known of the existence of the War Rooms. The Slab, for instance could not have been put in place without involving many workmen and there was always the need for routine maintenance and for occasional improvements. Such workmen and technicians would, however, have been sworn to secrecy and it was clearly the practice to use the same personnel for secret work so as to minimise the risk of indiscretion. William Heath, an electrician, spent nine months working on secret projects which included the installation of the scrambler phone that gave Churchill a direct line to Roosevelt secure for much of the time but penetrated by the Germans on at least one occasion, on 28 July 1943. He also helped install the scrambler machine in the basement of Selfridges department store in Oxford Street. Heath also worked in the tunnels under Dover Castle, which had played such an important part in the planning and conduct of the Dunkirk evacuation in 1940 and remained significant throughout – and indeed long after – the war. He told no-one, not even his wife or children, about his work but confided to his son Alan that he had sworn an oath of secrecy and that if he breached it he would be shot.[8]

In the troglodyte world of the War Rooms only the clock told whether it was night or day, and the state of the weather above ground was reported to those who worked there by a notice-board: an electric bell gave warning of an air-raid. The ever-present Royal Marine guards came to be taken for granted by the inhabitants but impressed visitors and new arrivals as they made their way down the steps leading to what some referred to as the 'Hole in the Ground'. 'Just like a waxwork', said one new secretary as she passed the guard standing half-way down the spiral staircase, but the waxworks soon revealed themselves as very human, teasing the women as they scurried up from the bedrooms below to the bathrooms clad in their dressing-gowns and with curlers in their hair. Mrs Joy Hunter, then a secretary, remembers that one guard was known to pass his spare time doing delicate embroidery.[9]

Here was an artificial environment, brightly lit by a combination of strip-lighting and hundreds of bulbs, with its air piped in from the rotundas, codenamed 'Anson', in Horseferry Road. These three circular concrete structures, built in spaces which had once contained gas-holders, housed a variety of organisations during the war, including parts of the Air Ministry, the Ministry of Home Security, and Home Office Fire Control. One had been considered as an alternative base for the War Cabinet and its secretariat, and was eventually kitted out to receive the prime minister. Beneath the steel and concrete crust of the rotundas lay connecting corridors with their own power plant, water supply and radio station. The rotundas were the life-support system, for their pumps sucked in air and piped it to the War Rooms, where it retained a distinctive scent of raw metal.

The CWR basement, thanks to the Slab, was protected, though not totally secure, from bombing. But there was another threat: flooding. A whole network of tunnels lies under Whitehall connecting the War Rooms to other government departments. Some are postwar, some are even now being worked on and others are centuries old. Many were constructed by the civil engineer William Halcrow in the 1930s. Plans for great tunnel shelters were never realised, but

Halcrow's Post Office tunnel carried cables between key departments including the Cabinet Office basement, No. 10 and the War Office, and the Whitehall Deep Tunnel to Horseferry Road was completed in August 1942. There was always the danger that, as the War Rooms lie beneath the level of the River Thames, bombing might result in water entering the tunnels and flooding passages and rooms. To guard against this, flood doors were fitted and pumps were installed.

Joan Bright (later Joan Bright Astley) moved to the War Rooms in December 1940 from the War Office, where she had worked for Military Intelligence. In her new post she was attached to the Joint Planning Committee under Lieutenant-Colonel Cornwall Jones. She describes a

> ... labyrinth of brightly lit and varnished rooms and passages, their air-conduit pipes gaily painted red ... In this warren were offices, conference rooms, canteens and bedrooms guarded and staffed by dark blue uniformed Royal Marines. The Joint Planning Staff, the Joint Intelligence Committee, the Strategical [*sic*] Planning Section, Future Operations Planning Section, the section devoted to thinking out the enemy's intentions, the section to produce ways of deceiving the enemy about projected operations, Colonel Combe and his code names – here they all were, dug down deep.[10]

The reshaping of the CWR

As a secure meeting place for the War Cabinet, the underground rooms had their heyday in the autumn and winter of 1940–41. Thereafter the War Cabinet usually met at 10 Downing Street or the House of Commons, with perhaps 115 sessions, about one in ten of its meetings, being held in the War Rooms during the course of the war. The chiefs of staff also preferred to meet elsewhere, usually upstairs in the NPO, after the worst of the Blitz was over.

The need for secure accommodation became important once more in 1943 as, although the Luftwaffe was no longer considered to have the resources to mount another Blitz, information arrived in August that Germany was preparing a new attack, this time using the V-weapons – flying bombs and rockets. Once more the suitability of the NPO as the command centre of the war was questioned. The Crossbow Committee was set up to evaluate defences against the new weapons and to ensure that the machinery of government could be kept running. It decided against reviving the 'Black Move' but recommended that citadel accommodation be investigated.[11] It was clear that the CWR was not safe against a 1100 lb bomb with a delayed-action fuse, and a survey of available citadels pointed to the Horseferry Road rotundas as the most suitable. Two possible options identified in late 1943 were:

(a) That the Cabinet Office continues to work where it is now, using the downstairs accommodation when there is a blitz, but that the PM, after dark, should be in say the citadel in Horseferry Road connected to the Cabinet Office by tunnel. Meetings of ministers or COS after dark would take place there.

(b) That the main business of the Cabinet Office

> transplants itself to the new citadel in Horseferry Road.[12]

In the end neither plan was implemented and the Cabinet Office continued to work where it was. When the attack by V1 flying bombs began in June 1944 the War Cabinet began to meet in the CWR once more, and held many meetings there until September, when fewer of the V1s were getting through. The risk had certainly been great. On 8 June a V1 hit the Guards Chapel on Birdcage Walk when it was packed for morning service: 122 of the congregation were killed and 141 seriously injured. But the first V2 rocket hit England on 8 September, and as the risk increased so the Cabinet often met underground until after the last V2 reached London on 28 March 1945.

From 1941 a number of factors changed both the configuration of the War Rooms and the use made of them. Increasingly rooms doubled up as emergency accommodation for senior personnel who worked mainly upstairs, space was vacated as Home Command HQ moved first to the CWR Annexe, where the Churchill Museum is today, and then on to Horseferry Road, and extra accommodation was required as the number of sections and committees under the umbrellas of Joint Planning and Joint Intelligence grew.

Rooms in the original basement were re-allocated. Thus Hollis was given as emergency accommodation the room previously allocated to Sir Findlay Stewart (69A), the senior civilian in Home Command. Room 67, no longer required by the chiefs, was assigned to the prime minister's Private Office staff, the room next to it (66B) went to John Martin, the principal private secretary, and Room 62 provided emergency accommodation for the personal secretaries and typists of the secretariat. The camp commandant (the officer responsible for the day-to-day administration of the place) moved into Room 63 and 62A became a mess for the Royal Marines, whose numbers had now grown to forty-nine.

Further south down this main corridor, rooms were also assigned to senior personnel, Bridges and Ismay and their private secretaries, to Lawrence Burgis and other members of the civil side of the secretariat, largely for emergency use, and to Colonel Capel-Dunn, secretary to the Joint Intelligence Committee. The War Cabinet switchboard moved for a time to the courtyard corridor but was eventually combined with the No. 10 Annexe switchboard and took over the whole of sub-divided Room 60, giving it three times its previous capacity.[13] Apart from the Map Room, the real nerve-centre of the War Rooms, the Mess in Room 68 and the switchboard, most of the corridor in the western basement was not in continuous use. One tiny room opposite the Map Room had an importance out of proportion to its size, for it was from there, behind the door with its 'Vacant' and 'Engaged' lock, leading casual passers-by to expect a wholly different function, that Churchill made his transatlantic phone calls.

Many of the courtyard rooms were similarly little occupied. They had been prepared during the Blitz for the prime minister, his wife, his personal staff, ministers and advisers and were maintained against a resumption of heavy bombing. That so many rooms were underused was entirely justifiable, for no-one could know when there might be a sudden and desperate need for them. What this meant, however, was that apart from the Map Room, its annexe and the switchboard, dynamic activity was transferred to CWR Annexe. The Joint Planning and Joint Intelligence staff grew in numbers as the war continued spawning new sections and committees. Until the Annexe was vacated by Home Command in 1942, they had been spread all over the NPO, but now they could be concentrated in the most discrete part of the building.

The displacement of Home Forces and increased numbers of the Joint Planning and Joint Intelligence staff in the War Rooms marked a significant shift in the focus of the war, as defence of the homeland gave way to planning for the invasion of French North Africa, Sicily, the Italian mainland and then France. The volume of work generated by the joint planners was prodigious. From the beginning to the end of the war the JPS produced plans for countless operations, many of which never got further than a carefully researched paper, which was dismissed by the chiefs of staff or the JPS Defence Committee, though others became the basis for entire campaigns. The JPS was a body which, as a recent study has declared, 'Churchill never came to like', largely because it pointed out the difficulty or impracticality of some of his favourite projects. He grumbled that it epitomised 'the whole machinery of negation'.[14] The Joint Intelligence Committee (JIC), chaired by Victor Cavendish-Bentinck (later 9th Duke of Portland), similarly laboured night and day, analysing intelligence information gathered from a multitude of sources including espionage and electronic eavesdropping, and met the chiefs of staff every Tuesday. It was in the nature of its task that the JIC was not always right – for instance, it was over-optimistic in concluding that German morale was crumbling in September 1944 – but its carefully researched and balanced reports were often dismissed by the chiefs on less than adequate grounds. Probably there were too many fingers in the intelligence pie: each service had its own intelligence section, while some sections came under the Ministry of Economic Warfare. Each single-service chief was sent Ultra decrypts, as, of course, was Churchill.

More specialised planning sections were formed. The Strategic Planning Staff (STRATS), the Executive Planning Staff (EPS), the Joint Administrative Planning Staff (JAPS), the Future Operational Planning Staff (FOPS) and later – and somewhat optimistically – the Post Hostilities Planning Staff (PHP). Joint Intelligence also expanded, dividing into Joint Intelligence Staff, the Interservices Security Board and Joint Intelligence Operations. The London Controlling Section was the undercover name for the Deception Planning Group, which devised plans for confusing and deceiving the enemy. Among its achievements was the creation of 'The Man Who Never Was', by dressing a corpse in the uniform of a Royal Marine major and attaching to it a briefcase containing false information about Britain's next objectives. The body and briefcase were slipped into the sea and, when washed ashore in Spain, the documents soon ended up in German hands and helped persuade the Germans into believing that there would be landings in Sardinia and Greece rather than Sicily. A massive deception plan, code-named Operation Fortitude, helped ensure that the Germans did not realise that the Allied invasion of 1944 would actually take place in Normandy. A small sub-set of this project was London Controlling Section's use of a Pay Corps lieutenant who bore a striking physical likeness to General Montgomery and was an actor before and after the war, to persuade the Germans that the 'general' was being fêted in notoriously leaky Gibraltar, encouraging them to believe that landings would take place in southern France before attempts were made elsewhere.

Literary dimensions

In his novel *The Military Philosophers,* Anthony Powell has his alter ego Nicholas Jenkins attend an Intelligence Committee meeting in the CWR. Jenkins is escorted down flights of stairs by a Royal Marine, whose '"Aye, aye, sir"... increased a sensation of going down below decks on a ship', to a 'room in the bowels of the earth', with fittings and decoration 'less down-at-heel than the general run of headquarters and government offices'. Powell describes the ethos of this underground world:

> In this brightly lit dungeon lurked a sense that no-one could spare a word, not a syllable, far less gesture, not of direct value in implementing the matter in hand. The power principle could almost be felt here, humming and vibrating like the drummings of the teleprinter. The sensation that resulted was oppressive, even a shade alarming.[15]

Powell was, for a short time, a military assistant secretary at the Cabinet Office, and so his description was based on experience. His appointment seems to have come about quite casually in March 1943 at the request of Lieutenant-Colonel Denis Capel-Dunn, secretary of the JIC, whom he had met briefly. Capel-Dunn was a formidable figure, whom Noel Annan, serving in the JIC, thought 'elusive and secretive'[16] and Joan Bright considered 'clever and strange'.[17] A barrister in civilian life, he was rated highly for his flair in drafting documents, a skill which a gifted writer like Powell should surely have shared.[18] Capel-Dunn was nicknamed the 'Papal Bun' by Powell's colleague in Military Intelligence Liaison, Captain Alick Dru, a play on his 'double-barrelled name, creed, demeanour, personal appearance'. Powell commented in his memoirs on Capel-Dunn's ability as the secretary of meetings:

> Where the often conflicting views of the three services and two government departments were in question, agreement was not always easily arrived at. Much argument could arise over the difference between what had been said, what set down in the 'paper'. The Bun was preternaturally gifted in bringing about acquiescence.[19]

Capel-Dunn's approval of Powell was quickly withdrawn. Powell thought him inconsiderate, but admits in his autobiography that 'to put it mildly, I was not at all a success in my new employment'.[20] His appointment lasted only nine weeks and he then returned to his former work with Military Intelligence Liaison, which involved dealing with the military representatives of allied and neutral governments. Capel-Dunn, however, lives on in Powell's writings, for he served as at least part of the model for his character Widmerpool.

That Powell did not exactly fit in with the ethos of the JIS or the War Rooms is demonstrated by comments in his autobiography. The JIS committees produced a continuous stream of papers on every aspect and sphere of the war and as secretary, usually assisting Capel-Dunn, he had to summarise the committees' conclusions, which, as committee might not finish until the early hours of the morning and the summaries of its discussions had to be ready for circulation the following morning, meant a long, often fourteen-hour, working day. Powell wondered 'whether the best results were always achieved by weary men poring over complicated documents night after night into the small hours'. He was also unimpressed by the importance attached to extreme secrecy. Knowledge of certain major operational matters might, he conceded, be useful to the enemy but he was somewhat sceptical as to whether much of the statistical material the committees pondered over and collated was actually all that important.[21]

Another novelist, Dennis Wheatley, whose books featuring satanism and the occult deprived me of many hours sleep when I was at school, had a longer and more successful career in the War Rooms.[22] In his early forties at the beginning of the war, Wheatley bombarded his contacts in Whitehall with papers setting out suggestions for the prosecution of the war. His paper on 'Resistance to Invasion' attracted the attention of Wing Commander Lawrence Darvell, who asked him to write a paper looking at invasion plans from a German point of view and to send it to 'Mr Rance's room in the Office of Works', which though Wheatley did not know it at the time, was the cover name for the joint planning staff's base in the CWR. He followed this up with two further papers on 'Further Measures for Resistance to Invasion' and 'Village Defence'. A man with enormous energy, he was to write some 500,000 words on various aspects of the war, and his fertile imagination hatched many ingenious and some astonishing plans. His bizarre concept of an Atlantic Life-Line, a huge assemblage of rafts tied together and impelled by the Gulf Stream to bring supplies to Scotland's Atlantic shore, was never put into practice, but then neither was the aircraft carrier made of artificial ice that Lord Mountbatten favoured, while the 'Mulberry' artificial harbours and the oil pipeline under the ocean (PLUTO), both used in Normandy, could easily have been dismissed as fanciful.

Wheatley and his formidable wife had a great network of social contacts: he was a generous host with a fine wine cellar,[23] and in December 1941 a place was found for him in the London Controlling Section based in the CWR Annexe and which, as we have seen, dealt with deception. He was commissioned into the RAFVR and was subsequently promoted wing commander. Along with Colonel J.H. Bevan, chief of the European Deception Section, he helped work out the cover plan for Operation 'Torch', the invasion of French North Africa, and was one of the seven staff officers who helped mislead the German High Command over where to expect the D-Day landings.

'The tattoo of high heels'

Pre-war Whitehall had adapted slowly to the employment of women, although the male clerk on the high stool had disappeared and the female shorthand typist at her desk replaced him. The civil service was, nevertheless, ahead of its time in offering entry to women secretaries via competitive examinations which led to secure employment, but in the War Office the typists were closely supervised by older women with scratchy pens who carefully monitored which officers they took dictation from most frequently, to prevent the formation of any dangerous liaisons. The concept of a woman as a personal assistant to a high-ranking officer and, thus, party to top secret information was almost inconceivable at the beginning of the war but within a year, as Joan Bright Astley has recorded:

> the rot had set in. By the time the bombs were really falling on England there was scarcely a senior officer without his female 'personal assistant' – a temporary civil servant for the duration – her high heels beating an efficient and provocative tattoo up and down the murky corridors, in and out of the shabby rooms.[24]

Joan Bright captures perfectly the impact that civilian women, at once efficient and feminine, had upon Whitehall at war and upon the secretariat in particular. She was exceptional, not only in the unique post she came to occupy as archivist to the chiefs of staff and commanders-in-chief and as the senior administrator of the British delegations to allied conferences, but in the exotic route through which she percolated to join the War Cabinet secretariat. Her recruitment to a secretive branch of military intelligence, specialising in ensuring that the Romanian oil fields did not fall into German hands, had, in time-honoured cloak and dagger fashion, involved waiting at St James's Park Underground Station while wearing a pink carnation, before being met by a woman who escorted her, with many changes of direction, to an anonymous office. On the outbreak of war her department, MI(R), lost the D categorisation, which denoted undercover work including spying and sabotage, and was moved to the War Office, where Joan spent the next year. She was fond of the War Office and her exciting work there, which had involved getting to know such glamorous figures as Peter and Ian Fleming and the actor David Niven. She occasionally went out with Ian Fleming, and, though she affirmed that had certainly been no torrid affair, is credited with being one of the models for the redoubtable Miss Moneypenny in the James Bond series. She was advised by her head of department, who was leaving for a new post, that the Cabinet Office was the place to be. After a discouraging interview with Ian Jacob, who told her that the Cabinet Office did not employ women as private secretaries, she had in August 1940 another interview with Lieutenant-Colonel Cornwall Jones, secretary of the JPS. This took place in Hatchett's basement restaurant in Piccadilly, popular because it was believed to be safe from bombing, 'to the thump-thump of a dance band', and she was offered a job on his staff and in December moved over to Great George Street.

Most of the typists reached the Cabinet Office by

conventional paths. Ilene Adams, having taken and passed the examination in shorthand and typing in Newcastle, moved to London at the beginning of the war and began work in the War secretariat at Richmond Terrace, an adventurous step for an eighteen-year-old. In 1940, she moved with the secretariat to the NPO and worked throughout the war at first in No. 10 Annexe, taking dictation from Bridges, Ismay and Hollis, and then for the JPS in the War Rooms. Gladys Hymer, also a shorthand typist in the civil service, was working for the Clearing Office, which dealt with foreign trade, at the beginning of the war. Foreign trade having become virtually non-existent, she was transferred in May 1941 to the CWR where she worked as a shorthand writer for the JPS.

It was because of Joan Bright that Olive Christopher came to work in the War Cabinet. Interviewed at the War Office, she was told to 'Ask for Miss Bright' and, though appointed as a secretary, was soon working in the Interservices Security Bureau, part of MO9, which among its other activities recruited agents, including David Niven, who, at the time of the Dunkirk evacuation picked up stragglers and brought them back from France and later served as a lieutenant-colonel in 'Phantom', the GHQ liaison regiment. One of 'the girls', as the able temporary civil servants in the War Office were known, Olive, at Joan Bright's suggestion, applied for transfer to the offices of the War Cabinet and worked in the CWR. She found herself typing the minutes of late night meetings which had to be ready for distribution early the following morning, and with the expansion of the JPS the workload was increasing. Everyone hated the Gestetner copiers which were used to roll off copies for distribution. Rather bored with her work, she applied, with Joan Bright's help, for a position with MI5. Mr Winnifreth, the personnel officer in the War Rooms, refused to release her, and early in 1943 she joined Jacqueline d'Orville as a second secretary to Brigadier Hollis.

Jacqueline d'Orville (later Lady Iliff) worked for the Home Office at the beginning of the war and moved to the Cabinet Office at the same time as Norman Brook in 1941. She became Hollis's secretary and worked mainly on the second floor. Hollis, she remembers, spent most of his working day there but would go down to the CWR after he came back from his club, do some more work and sleep there. His other secretary, Olive Christopher, divided her time between the upstairs office and Hollis's other office in the CWR.[25]

Wendy Wallace (later Wendy Maxwell) served longest in the secretariat. Previously in the Foreign Office, she joined the CID in 1938 and thus witnessed the preparations for war, the establishment of the War Cabinet and the beginning of Churchill's premiership. During the Blitz, she would be down in the CWR for the 9 p.m. Defence Committee meeting and later spend the early hours of the morning typing up the minutes before going to bed in the basement 'Dock'.[26]

It was not only the number of women working in the War Cabinet secretariat and in the service departments that distinguished Britain's command centre from those of other allied powers, but the number of *civilian* women. When the British delegations arrived in Moscow and Washington, they found an array of women in uniform. Ismay and Hollis were proud of their smartly dressed civilian female staff, found them efficient and liked the contribution they made to the atmosphere of the office:

> 'You don't put your girls in uniform then?' remarked General Eisenhower one day,
>
> 'It wouldn't make them any more reliable if we did', said General Hollis.[27]

Into the secretariat had moved, not a monstrous regiment of women, but a flotilla of efficient, intelligent, poised and fashionably dressed young women. They changed immediately the atmosphere of what had been the CID. Joan Bright did much to establish the position of the women, who became temporary civil servants. She had the poise and confidence to make it plain that female staff had distinct positions and responsibilities as much as military officers and male civil servants. When working 'downstairs' for JPS, she was asked by the then Major Anthony Head to take dictation, and at once refused. She was neither a clerk nor a stenographer, and the girls who were would resent her taking away their work. Joan Bright also created a unique position for herself. With her systematic mind, she was able to marshal a mass of complex documents within the clear and accessible filing systems she designed, and this led to the suggestion, put to her by Ismay over lunch, that she move upstairs and set up an information room for visiting commanders-in-chief. Eventually she agreed and moved up to the second floor, where she created, not just a room where generals, admirals and air marshals could update themselves on different spheres of the war in which they were not directly concerned, but somewhere they could do so in a relaxed atmosphere.

Miss Bright, charming and knowledgeable, became a confidante of the great and good. When Wavell, relieved of his command in the Middle East and appointed CinC India, came in, she took him down below to meet her old colleagues in the JPS and the Map Room. He took her off to lunch, and walking back through St James's Park, asked: 'Why does Winston dislike me, Joan?' It was a question she could not really answer truthfully without further hurting Wavell's already bruised feelings, and she avoided doing so, but the fact that Wavell asked her is revealing. It demonstrates Joan Bright's reputation for being at the heart of the 'Inner Circle' as well as the integrity she exuded, and also hints at how men will confide in women in a way that they rarely will in other men. It is unlikely that Wavell would have put this question to a man who was not his equal in rank, even if he was as trustworthy as Joan.

The secretariat, upstairs and downstairs, the prime minister's office and even his family and personal attendants made up what was in practice a single organisation. There were doors between one section and another, especially the well-guarded door that led to the underground rooms, but it was essentially one world and women were integral to its whole structure and atmosphere.

In the secretariat everyone worked hard, and the pressures were great. Operations were planned and undertaken, and then there was anxiety as word came through of success or failure: all were conscious of the importance and urgency of the tasks in hand. The women who worked there recalled long hours and late nights, often followed by a descent to uncomfortable sleeping quarters in the Dock, but their enduring memories are of the sheer excitement of the work, the relaxed relations between senior and junior staff and the camaraderie among the female staff.

The ethos came from the top, for Ismay was only interested in the best: the best people and the best work, and he got the very best out of his staff by skilful and friendly management.

There was, of course, a hierarchy among the female staff just as there was among the men. Women worked both upstairs and downstairs, but those who tended to end up on the second floor had been picked out as particularly able and reliable. This was where Ismay, Hollis and Jacob had their main offices. In the large central office, between the rooms of Ismay and Hollis, worked their secretaries and personal assistants: among them, Betty Green, Mollie Brown, Olive Christopher, Jacqueline d'Orville, Margaret Sutherland, Wendy Wallace, Sylvia Arnold and Margaret Fairlie. Members of this group bonded tightly, and with Joan Bright, who in many cases had been responsible for recognising their abilities, not only became friends during the war but remained close for long afterwards. Other, more junior, secretaries were based in two rooms for typists and stenographers, one upstairs and one downstairs.

Both Ismay and Hollis liked having women working for them, flirted in a harmless enough way and enjoyed the different atmosphere that their presence brought to wartime command. In return, female assistants were proud of their bosses. Olive Christopher would refer to 'my Brigadier' and then 'my General' and, after Hollis was knighted, to his wife as 'Lady Jo', while, as we have seen, she would call him

'Jo' in private. Ismay was relaxed, and within the inner circle there was little use of rank or title when senior officers and civil servants addressed each other. This rather disturbed Churchill, who sent a crusty memo to Ismay and Bridges demanding that private secretaries and others should stop addressing each other by their first names when writing on matters of an official character.[28]

The attitudes of Ismay and Hollis to their female staff would, no doubt, horrify later feminists: 'There goes a fine filly', said Ismay of Jacqueline d'Orville and, when Olive Christopher was interviewed by Hollis, he followed up his question about her shorthand and typing skills with 'May I say what very fine legs you have' – certainly not a comment applauded by modern interviewing guidelines. But, as Joanna Moody has observed, the flirtation 'never really meant anything and anyway they were a bit flattered'.[29] General Jacob was very different, as Joan Bright Astley tells us in *The Inner Circle*. Impressed by the fact that the Americans seemed to have only uniformed staff, he thought to replace his 'witty and Scottish Miss Wendy Wallace' with an army corporal, without imagining the blow this would be to her self-esteem and to her regard for him. He was forced to surrender, and Miss Wallace swept back in triumph.[30]

Jacob had meant no harm but he lacked the sensitivity to the feelings of others that was the forte of Ismay and Hollis. Dedicated to his work, he approached the war in the same remorselessly professional spirit that he might have applied to a peacetime army exercise. At its end he told Joan Bright: 'What an interesting war you've had Joan. I just seem to have been to the office and to my club.'[31] This is not to underestimate his contribution to the secretariat for, though he seemed cool and undemonstrative, his concentrated intelligence was a major asset and under his tough exterior beat a warm heart. Once someone had pierced his reserve, there could be no more loyal friend and supporter. Wendy Wallace (later Maxwell) recounts that he was a wonderful man, a lifelong friend, who would give her advice on every step she made. Churchill, she affirms, trusted and relied upon his judgement.[32]

The senior secretaries and personal assistants formed a close-knit and mutually supportive group. As within any organisation employing hundreds of people, there were divisions and sub-divisions of respect and affection and small groups of really close friends. Down in the War Rooms were not only more typists and stenographers but the telephone operators. Rose Gibbs (later Haynes) was told in 1942 that she was being transferred to an unknown telephone exchange. She had to sign a national secrecy document, and was given a special pass and instructions as to where to find this secret exchange. Down in the CWR she found the switch room, not much different in appearance from other telephone exchanges but 'all these calls were scrambled so we never knew who we were connecting to who. No 999 calls here, every call was treated as urgent.' The recreation room for the telephone operators of this exchange, code-named 'Federal', was built over the foundations of the kitchen of the old royal Palace of Whitehall, destroyed by fire in the seventeenth century, and was reputed to be haunted. It had a full-size table-tennis table, and 'When we were on night duty about 2 a.m., we could hear Charles the Second [or Charley Two, as he was nicknamed] playing table tennis, the tennis ball was tapping as it was hitting the table to and fro. It was of course the air conditioning playing tricks with our minds.'[33] The telephone operators did not help their nerves by playing with a ouija board. If only they had known, Dennis Wheatley was an expert in matters supernatural, the basis of many of his best-sellers, and worked only a few yards away.

The code and cypher officers

The women who worked in the secretariat were all civilians, but the war's command centre depended on a small detachment of women in uniform. In 1942, the Cabinet Office and chiefs of staff decided that a Cypher Office for their use should be set up by the RAF in order to coordinate all signals formerly handled by the separate services. From April that year a section of Women's Auxiliary Air Force (WAAF) officers under the command of Squadron Officer Joan Williams played a crucial role in encoding and decoding all signals entering and leaving the NPO.

She had been in charge of the Air Ministry Cypher Office and was asked to set up the Air Ministry Special Signals Office, which became the Cabinet Office Cypher Office in 1943, when it was moved to the ground floor of the NPO. Ian Jacob explained her section's duties to her in March 1942 and ordered her to select her team of officers. Eight were required as there were to be four watches, each covered by two officers. All incoming messages had to be decoded and then typed and copied before being sent to the Cabinet Office. Joan Williams recollects that 'In a matter of weeks, the officers were chosen, the books, typex [the machines which coded and decoded messages] and typewriters arrived and on 13th April, we started.'

Duties in the Cypher Office were arduous: the amount of work increased, and conditions in the larger office in the sub-basement that the unit was moved to were poor as it was dusty and almost airless. It was guarded by one of the elderly security staff, who stood half-way down the staircase and had a locked 'stable door' over which all visitors, however senior, had to present their passes. Late in the summer of 1943 there was a move to better quarters and the cypher officers were installed in four rooms adjoining the prime minister's ground-floor Map Room and the entrance to the Churchills' flat. Joan Williams recalls that this was 'a great joy for here we had plenty of fresh air and an outlook onto St James's Park'.

Although the Cabinet Office Cypher Office was made up of WAAF officers and was technically under Air Ministry command, it was part of the Cabinet Office secretariat and therefore controlled by Ismay, Hollis and Jacob, Captain Clifford and Air Commodore Earl, all of whom reported directly to the prime minister. Leslie Hollis had overall responsibility for the effectiveness of the cypher arrangements. He had not met Squadron Officer Williams when he called for the officer in charge after a message marked 'All Most Secret and Personal for Chiefs of Staff' was circulated to all on the normal 'Secret' distribution list. Hollis told his private secretary, Mr Jones, to find the officer responsible, saying: 'Send for him at once. I will take the pants off him!' In due course Mr Jones reported to Hollis that Squadron Leader Williams had arrived:

> In a loud and angry voice I told him to show the officer in. I was taken aback when I was confronted with a beautiful and bewitching young lady. I begged her to be seated and suggested that tears were unnecessary. She expressed the deepest concern over the mistake which, of course, was not of her own making. Seeing that the poor girl was feeling the strain, I said something to the effect that, although mistakes must not happen again the incident should be regarded as closed provided the necessary reprimands to those concerned were issued. The Squadron Leader was still a bit overcome, and when finally taking her departure a tear or two came into her eyes. When an army officer asked what the Brigadier had been doing to make Miss Williams cry, Mr Jones replied that he had overheard the Brigadier say he 'was going to take the pants off somebody.'[34]

Joan Williams insists that she never denied that the mistake was hers, adding confidently that 'I don't think he reduced me to tears.'

The Cypher Office grew in size throughout the war, and by its end Joan Williams was in charge of forty-eight officers, a very high degree of responsibility for an officer who continued in the rank she held when it was first set up. She was fiercely proud of 'my girls', as she continues to call them, and supported them consistently. Her office was treated rather unfairly by the RAF in terms of promotions for it was technically part of the establishment of RAF Leighton Buzzard, and this included responsibility for pay and promotion. The office's importance was, however, fully recognised by the Cabinet Office and the chiefs-of-staff, who relied on it absolutely. Joan Williams was appointed OBE in 1944, an honour she regards as a tribute to her section.

The Code and Cypher Office was essential to the complex that made up the Cabinet Office, for communication security was vital, a fact underlined by the advantage that Ultra conferred upon Britain. Important phone calls made by Churchill and others were scrambled, eventually by a device so big that it had to be housed in the basement of Selfridges, but messages sent by telegraph had to be coded and decoded, a complex and laborious process involving special machines attached to typewriters. It was rather lonely work, with little of the sociability to be found in the rest of Storey's Gate. The WAAF officers were closeted with each other and worked a series of shifts and had little chance either to see anyone from other departments or meet the many young officers they passed in the corridor on the way from the Great George Street entrance to their guarded workplace. That excellent morale was maintained in these circumstances was remarkable.

Danger laced with fun

Nobody hearing or reading the recollections of those who worked in London during the war can fail to be struck by the sharp contrasts of daily experience. The everyday journey to work, the hours at the office or shop or the evening at the pub were as normal except for the intrusion of abnormality in the shape of the bomb, or later the 'doodlebug' or rocket. There was austerity, rationing and often sudden shortages, perhaps of beer or some ordinary foodstuff. As a norm one queued, and then rushed to a particular shop when it was rumoured that some rare delight was obtainable briefly. Yet people continued to enjoy themselves, and pubs, clubs and dance-halls were full. Perhaps pleasures were sharpened by the fact that there was always a risk of death and relationships made more urgent by the war's unpredictable character.

Few moved through London, bomb-damaged but demonstrably getting on with business and pleasure, into the very centre of the war's management in the same way as those who worked in the NPO. Few emerged blinking into the daylight from a world of artificial light and imported air with the gratitude of those who spent long nights in the CWR. One had to be psychologically and physically robust to cope. William Heath, who helped install the electrical system, said the CWR were very damp and the ventilation poor: his skin broke out in a rash that he blamed on the conditions. Myra Collyer, who worked as a shorthand typist, describes compulsory sunlamp treatment to counteract the effects of working underground: one colleague took off her protective glasses, and nearly lost her sight. As the ashtrays which are now such a marked feature of the War Rooms suggest, almost everyone smoked: Cabinet meetings generated a great fug with Churchill's cigars, Attlee's pipe and Bevin's endless cigarettes. The smell of cooking lingered, there were malodorous whiffs from the Elsan toilets, and when Myra Collier put a handkerchief over a ventilation outlet it came back black with soot.

The NPO were no more dangerous than most places in the capital and, indeed, during the Blitz, central London took less of a pounding than the East

End and the City. Bombs did fall on Whitehall, one on Clive Steps, just outside the CWR and very close to its present entrance, and Ilene Adams remembered 'One girl killed by shrapnel as she went out of the office door'. Rose Gibb was on duty when the first doodlebug was dropped (in Bethnal Green, east London) and 'nobody knew what they were ... the switchboard came alight, everyone was trying to reach somebody to find out what was going on'. All staff had to double up as ARP (Air Raid Precautions) wardens. Still, they felt safe in the CWR, and even on the upstairs floors of the NPO there was always the knowledge that there was shelter in the basements.

What was probably more frightening for many staff was going home and spending a night listening to the bombs fall. Joan Bright had already been bombed out once when her flat in Curzon Street was hit, and was living in St Ermin's Hotel just across the park from Storey's Gate when she awoke one night 'to a bedroom glowing red, fitfully red; the church across the road was on fire'. Olive Christopher lived in Croydon, though she usually slept in the Dock, but one night received a call to say that her home had been firebombed. She also just escaped, by the luck of a cancelled date, the direct hit on the Café de Paris which killed eighty people.

Night clubs, gentlemen's clubs in St James's, pubs and cinemas were all bombed, yet people kept having a good time, and wartime London maintained a feverish glamour. 'I suppose I shouldn't say so', comments Lady Iliff, née d'Orville, 'but we had a lot of fun. When you're young you don't worry about danger.' Wendy Maxwell agrees that with all the horror and the austerity there was excitement and a good social life. There might be gaps where shops had been, and food might be plain, boring and rationed, though, until late in 1942, restaurants could often provide elaborate meals. Clothes had to be bought with coupons as well as money, but many women still managed to dress fashionably. The girls in the secretariat were both ingenious and mutually supportive, making and altering their own and each others' clothes and always on the look-out for the unexpected bargain or a dress or a coat that they knew would suit a colleague's taste and fitting. After nights spent sleeping in the Dock with the hum of the air-conditioning and the scuttle of rats, and with days of endless note-taking and typing before them, they would emerge from the bathroom looking as glamorous as possible. From 1942 onwards, however, there was to be, at least for some, an unexpected bonus to life in the secretariat: foreign travel.

5

THE BUNKER GOES ABROAD

Winston Churchill was always restless. He disliked being stuck in any one place for too long and had always been a great traveller. He first came under fire (accompanying Spanish forces in Cuba) in 1895, and even before he became a Member of Parliament in 1900, aged just twenty-six, he had already written two best-selling books, one based on his experiences on the North-West Frontier of India and the other on the 1898 campaign in the Sudan. During the war there was far more to his travelling than simple wanderlust. He believed that personal intervention could make a real difference and that meeting face-to-face with both allied leaders and British commanders enabled him to gauge moods, assess personalities and foster confidence and trust. In his first weeks as prime minister he flew to France five times in May and June 1940 to try and stiffen the resistance of the flagging French government and its outpaced army. In early 1942, Pug Ismay warned General Sir Claude Auchinleck, commander-in-chief in the Middle East, that Churchill's character meant that there was really no substitute for a personal meeting with the man:

> You cannot judge the PM by ordinary standards, he is not in the least like anyone you and I have ever met. He is a mass of contradictions. He is either on the crest of a wave, or in a trough; either highly laudatory, or bitterly condemnatory; either in an angelic temper or a hell of a rage; when he isn't fast asleep he's a volcano. There are no half measures in his make-up – he apparently sees no difference between harsh words spoken to a friend and forgotten within the hour under the influence of friendly argument, and the same harsh words telegraphed to a friend thousands of miles away – with no opportunity for making it up.[1]

For the rest of 1940 and for most of 1941, Churchill was confined to Britain but not to Whitehall. His special train, fitted out as a temporary headquarters and hotel-cum-office, enabled him to travel around the country visiting military units, airfields and ports, inspecting defences and providing a reassuring presence in areas that had suffered heavy bombing. Never concerned about his personal security, he would be accompanied by Inspector Thompson and a handful of officials, and, though often visibly moved by what he saw, neither appeared downcast nor sought to be shielded from shocked survivors. Historian Geoffrey Best contrasts this behaviour with that of Hitler, 'who never allowed himself to be seen visiting bomb-damaged German cities', adding that: 'Nothing did more to maintain popular morale under bombardment and other hardships than the knowledge that the residents of Buckingham Palace and Downing Street were sitting it out like all other Londoners.'[2] If anything was needed to justify the construction of the CWR, surely it was this. Churchill was especially fond of going to Dover, where he would gaze at the distant French coastline, roam around the castle's tunnels and fortifications and inspect another brain-child, a fourteen-inch gun that could shell the French coast.[3]

During the period when invasion was expected and British cities were being regularly bombed, it was inconceivable that the prime minister should leave Britain and, in any case, until June 1941 there were no allied leaders to meet. Even after Hitler had invaded Russia, there was, at first, no point in a meeting with Stalin while the Soviet Union's very existence was in doubt.

The voyage to Placentia Bay in August 1941 was the first of a series of Churchill's major wartime journeys. The hope of American intervention was his obsession, and the invitation from Roosevelt to a meeting at sea too good a chance to miss. It provided an opportunity for him to consolidate the relationship he felt he had established by letters and in his long conversations with the president's emissaries. The meeting was only modestly successful from Churchill's point of view, but in December came the Japanese attack on Pearl Harbor and thenceforth he took every opportunity to meet first Roosevelt, and then Stalin too.

Almost immediately after Japan's entry into the

war he was writing to the King (more evidence of his punctilious regard for the monarch) requesting permission to fly to Washington and directing Ismay to make the appropriate arrangements. Roosevelt was not particularly eager to be visited as, understandably, he was rather busy and tried to put Churchill off until he had had time to oversee America's mobilisation. He relented, and Churchill and a considerable retinue sailed on 13 December 1941 aboard HMS *Duke of York*.

This ushered in a period of intensive travel. In June 1942 Churchill was in Washington again, and from then until the end of the war he was often on the move, flying to Cairo, Moscow and Teheran in August, to Casablanca in the following January and making a further four journeys in 1943 to Washington (May), Quebec (August), Cairo (November) and Teheran (November–December). The autumn and early winter of 1944 saw him in Quebec again in September and then in Moscow (October) and Athens (December), while in 1945 he attended the Yalta Conference (February) and, after the end of the war in Europe, the Potsdam Conference (July), so aptly code-named 'Terminal'.

Churchill was by far the greatest traveller among the allied leaders and the most intrepid into the bargain. He went to both Washington and Moscow, but there was never any conference of allied leaders in London. Considering Roosevelt's infirmity, well disguised though it was from the American public, the president travelled considerable distances to allied conferences, going to Casablanca, Cairo, Teheran and Yalta. Stalin, who had only left Russia once, in April–May 1907, when he attended a Russian Social Democratic Labour Party conference in London, was the most reluctant to travel. Whether this was because of fear of flying, his health or a well-justified paranoia, which made him fear a coup if he was away too long, is uncertain, but he only ventured from Soviet-controlled territory to attend the Teheran Conference. He referred to Churchill as 'that desperate fellow who was always flying around the world'.[4] Perhaps Churchill was indeed desperate, for his relief that the war would not be lost was increasingly accompanied by dark realisation that the rewards of victory would be meagre for Britain. The USA and the Soviet Union could rely upon their industrial and military might to confirm their position in a post-war world. Churchill clung to the slim hope that his eloquence, and the relationships he had forged with Roosevelt and Stalin, could save Britain from loss of her great power status.

Whether all Churchill's travels resulted in benefits that outweighed the risks can be questioned. Journeys by sea were undoubtedly dangerous. Battleships like HMS *Prince of Wales, Duke of York* and *King George V* were capable of high speed and were shielded by armour, but when Churchill made his second visit to Roosevelt on *Duke of York,* the *Prince of Wales* had just been sunk by Japanese aircraft, a fact which concentrated the minds of those who had sailed to Placentia Bay aboard her and now found themselves in the familiar surroundings of a sister ship. If German intelligence had learned that a battleship was carrying Churchill, then U-boats might have lain in wait or bombers been dispatched. That speed was considered vital is shown by the use of the battle-cruiser HMS *Renown,* thinly armoured but the fastest capital ship in the fleet, to bring Churchill back from Quebec in August 1943 and, more strikingly, by the use of the liner *Queen Mary* to take him there as she had previously carried him to Washington in May. A passenger liner might seem a dangerous way to transport a prime minister and his staff across sea lanes in which wolf-packs of U-boats lurked. Yet although the *Queen Mary*, used as a troopship during the war, carried only light guns, she was fast and boasted an array of water-tight compartments. Relying on speed, a zig-zag course and secrecy, together with the protection offered by escorting cruisers and an aircraft carrier, she was probably as safe as a battleship – and infinitely more comfortable.

The perils of wartime air travel were underlined by the number of prominent people who died either in crashes or by being shot down. Aircraft transporting the prime minister were relatively safe once out over the western Atlantic, but while leaving or approaching Britain they were vulnerable to German fighters, and even the best security could not rule out 'friendly fire'. Flights close to the Mediterranean were in danger of encountering enemy fighters. Lieutenant-General 'Strafer' Gott, who Churchill had decided was to replace General Auchinleck at the head of the Eighth Army, was killed in August 1942, when his plane was shot down on its way to Cairo following the very route that Churchill had just flown.

There was another major disadvantage in flying: the risk to the prime minister's health. Transport in a battleship could be uncomfortable at high speed in heavy seas, but accommodation was relatively spacious and the voyage could even be relaxing. In comparison, a bomber like the Liberator, in which he flew to Cairo, Teheran and Moscow in 1942, could be uncomfortable and cold. Churchill was in his late sixties and was not a fit man. His doctor, Sir Charles Wilson (later Lord Moran), was much concerned at the risk flying posed to his health, and his advisers, staff and senior generals were all well aware that, although Churchill seemed indomitable, his health had broken down several times.

It was safest to fly at high altitude, but the aircraft of the day, even the comfortable and spacious Boeing sea planes, built for the peacetime 'Clipper' service (in which Churchill returned from America in January 1942 and flew there and back in June), lacked pressurised cabins, and to fly at over 10,000 feet was unwise for someone in Churchill's state of health. In 1943, he was provided with a personal plane, an Avro York, a conversion from the Lancaster bomber, which was much more comfortable than the Liberator, and in 1944 a Douglas C-54 Skymaster was made available by the Americans. British delegations had felt like poor relations, arriving at conferences crumpled and bleary-eyed, while their US counterparts stepped, crisp and fresh, out of grand Skymasters, but the fact that the only adequate planes came from the USA symbolised the increasing disparity between the power of the two nations.[5]

Colville's sardonic comment about Churchill's retinue rivalling Cardinal Wolsey's was apt, for the prime minister was usually accompanied by rather more generals, admirals and air marshals than were strictly necessary, while his personal entourage of private and personal secretaries together with his valet and detective made up a peregrinating court. He could rough it if he had to, but he preferred a grander progress in as much comfort as possible.

The size of the British delegations to the major wartime conferences was, in general, amply justified. That so many of the British wishes were met at the Casablanca Conference of January 1943 owed much to the meticulous preparations by the secretariat and chiefs of staff and the expertise brought to the conference by planners and advisers. The British had taken much of the command centre at the NPO with them. The Americans had done less preparation and brought only a small party of advisers. As General George C. Marshall later admitted: 'The British had a large staff; they brought along a ship for them to use. I had few people with me so I was shooting off the hip.' Andrew Roberts observes that: 'The Americans would not allow it to happen again.'[6]

By November 1943, his map-master Captain Pim calculated that Churchill had already travelled 110,000 miles since the outbreak of war. The strain put upon Churchill's health by his constant travels made Sir Charles Wilson an ever more important member of the entourage. During his visit to Washington in December 1941, the prime minister had a minor heart attack, and in Tunis in December 1943 he went down with pneumonia. Being Churchill's doctor was in many ways an even more daunting task than being his detective, for he was not inclined to take advice and was a decidedly grumpy patient. Lord Moran, as Wilson became in 1943, was an assiduous keeper of a diary and published it in 1966 as *Winston Churchill: The Struggle for Survival.* Seen by the Churchill family as a betrayal of a patient's trust, it detailed not only

Churchill's physical illnesses but the terrible bouts of depression – his 'Brown Hours' as Churchill himself called them – from which he suffered. Churchill did indeed show signs of exhaustion towards the end of the war, due in large part to frustration with the allies and at Britain's declining ability to control developments, but his determination and capacity for recovery were alike very impressive.

From the beginning, Churchill's travels were at once an opportunity and a headache for the secretariat and the chiefs of staff. Who should go, and who should stay behind? How could secure communications with the absent prime minister and his companions be maintained? The prime minister was the leader and the secretariat and chiefs of staff the nerve centre of operations and policy. To split the two was difficult.

'How I hated being left behind', admitted Ismay, left in charge when Churchill went to Washington in December 1941. There was, inevitably, an air of despondency in the Cabinet Office when the leader departed, taking with him a section of the secretariat and, usually, the chiefs. Off went the lucky ones, excited by the prospect of travel, the drama of allied conferences and escape from rationing and the blackout, leaving behind them an organisation which drew so much of its purpose and vitality from the prime minister. The work of the remaining planning and intelligence staff continued as usual and the Map Room was as scrupulously updated as ever, but on the upper floors there were empty offices and there was no angry rumble from the No. 10 Annexe. The workload of those left behind probably increased while prime minister and senior team were away. The prime ministerial delegations remained connected to the Whitehall base by scrambled telephone, coded dispatches and telegrams, and there was constant signals traffic from North Africa, the United States, the Middle East, Canada or Russia. At Casablanca, Ian Jacob declared that, thanks to the communications provided by the headquarters ship, HMS *Bulolo*, subsequently a headquarters ship on D-Day: 'We could operate exactly as if we were in Great George Street.'

It was usual for at least one of the senior members of the military and civil branches of the secretariat to remain behind. On the military side, the job of 'looking after the shop' usually fell to Hollis, who did not attend the important Casablanca and Yalta Conferences. Although Ismay did not get to Cairo and Moscow, his emollient presence was usually found necessary by both Churchill and the chiefs, but the indefatigable and the hyper-efficient Ian Jacob, exactly the right man for the prime minister or chiefs to have to hand when searching for a detail, and the most efficient of committee secretaries, attended most conferences.

It was also, until the Washington Conference of May 1943, deemed impossible for female staff to accompany the delegations. The Royal Navy was only just coming to terms with allowing uniformed women to travel aboard His Majesty's Ships and firmly declared that the passage of civilian women was wholly out of the question. As Joan Bright memorably put it: "'Civilian women should not go in battleships" sang the Board of Admiralty. Behind them swelled in harmony a chorus of generations of men of the Royal

Navy who had guarded their ships as jealously as they had guarded our shores.'[7] Accommodating women passengers in the inconvenient discomfort of a Liberator was, with more reason, considered impossible.

The secretaries and PAs in the Cabinet Office and No. 10 Annexe were bitter at their exclusion from the prime minister's entourage. Those who worked for Ismay, Hollis and Jacob were part of a close team, trusted with secrets and sure that they could do a better job for their superiors than any uniformed replacements, male or female. They had bonded with 'their generals', at least two decades older than they were, and regarded them as slightly glamorous, avuncular figures. 'Their generals' shared the view that their usual secretaries would do the most efficient job for them, but none went to Casablanca. Elizabeth Layton, personal secretary to the prime minister, similarly found herself excluded. When Churchill set off in the *Prince of Wales* for Placentia Bay, 'for dictation purposes a young man from another government department, Patrick Kinna, was roped in. No females – good Heavens, no!'[8] On the visit to Washington in December 1941 it was again Patrick Kinna and a RAF sergeant who went.

Their exclusion from the Casablanca Conference led, not unnaturally, to ill-feeling among the women of the secretariat towards the uniformed women who were in attendance: 'In our civilian clothes we typed, flagged, tagged, filed, slapping the papers into folders and feeling nasty about the girls in khaki and blue who would do the same at the other end.'[9] On their return, the generals' thoughtless chatter about smart servicewomen did not go down well. Here were two different tribes, both establishing themselves in the hitherto male world of war, the one striving ingeniously to retain feminine chic in a world of coupons and shortages, the other with ranks and uniforms.

One group of uniformed women working for the Cabinet Office also stayed behind and had to deal with a much-increased workload the WAAF Code and Cypher officers. As the then Squadron Officer Joan Williams observes:

> The first conference with which we had to deal started in August 1942 when the prime minister went to Cairo to review the Middle East Command set-up and then to Moscow for discussions with Marshal Stalin. This was our first conference and immediately there was a large increase in signals resulting in high pressure and necessitation for all officers on watch overlapping for an extra hour.[10]

The Washington Conference ('Trident') of May 1943 put immense pressure upon the WAAF Code and Cypher Officers. All watches stayed on double time for they were dealing with Anthony Eden's dispatches to the Foreign Office as well as the Cabinet Office signals, and Joan Williams worked thirty-six hours at a stretch. The Quebec Conference ('Quadrant') of August–September 1943 put a further strain on them. Immured in their guarded office, the WAAF officers had to work on the signals of the prime minister and chiefs of staff. Privy to some of the most closely guarded secrets, they maintained a low profile and led a lonely existence but knew just how much their work was valued by Ismay, Hollis and Jacob.

Nineteen forty-three was, in Ismay's words, 'Conference Year. In January there was Casablanca; in May, Washington; in August, Quebec; in October, Moscow (Conference of Foreign Ministers); in November, Cairo (Conference with the Turks); in November and December, Cairo and Teheran.' The meetings took place against the background of major developments which would predicate not just the course of the war but the future shape of the world.

Churchill's euphoria at the news of Pearl Harbor in December 1941 was justified. The long-term indicators suggested that Germany and her allies were unlikely to withstand the economic and military resources that were now piling up against them. The German army might be the best in the world, but the amazing output from the industrial–military complex of an America now gearing up for war, and the totalitarian ruthlessness of the Soviet war machine would be decisive in the end. The first half of 1942 was, nevertheless, not a good year for the British Empire: the humiliating surrender of Singapore was unquestionably the army's nadir; there were reverses in North Africa (a major theatre to the British but merely a side-show to the Germans) and the ineptly planned Dieppe Raid wasted many Canadian and British lives. In the autumn, however, El Alamein gave the British something to cheer about at last, and the US Navy's victory at Midway in June marked the turn of the tide in the Pacific.

The conferences of 1943 were, therefore, held against a much more positive background. The course of the war in Europe became clearer with the German surrender at Stalingrad and, arguably more importantly, the outcome of the great tank battle at Kursk in July, which put an end to German hopes of victory in the east. By September American and British forces had landed on the Italian mainland and Italy had surrendered. The Germans, characteristically deft in adversity, redeployed so as to defend Italy yard by yard, and instead of finding themselves stabbing up into the soft under-belly of Europe, as Churchill unwisely called it, the Allies were instead confronted with a tough old gut.

The Casablanca Conference of January 1943 stood on the very cusp of these changing fortunes (surrender at Stalingrad took place at the end of the month) and when Britain was still the senior partner to the USA in the European theatre. Britain had more forces in Europe and North Africa than her American ally, and El Alamein had redeemed the battered reputation of her army. A central issue in Anglo-American discussions was when to launch an invasion of France, the 'Second Front' which the Russians and, no less to the point, their supporters within the Western Alliance were loudly demanding. Military realism and British interests were at first against such an invasion, though an appreciable section of British public opinion, urged on by the unlikely combination of the Communist Party and the Beaverbrook press, was in favour. The task of Churchill and Alan Brooke was to persuade the Americans that landings in France were unlikely to succeed until Germany was much weaker and that operations in the Mediterranean would, for the time being, be more rewarding. The Americans took some convincing, suspecting that Britain was pursuing her own interests, but were themselves divided as to how resources should be allocated between the Pacific and Europe. By and large Churchill and Brooke were successful, and plans for landings in France, shelved in 1942, were again postponed. The Allied invasion of French North Africa, Operation 'Torch', was making progress, albeit slowly, and Roosevelt was persuaded to support, for the moment, the British policy of concentrating on the Mediterranean. It was decided to go ahead with the invasion of Sicily. There were heated discussions at Casablanca, and this was the last time that Churchill's persuasion and Brooke's forthrightness triumphed. The Washington Conference that May was to prove far harder for the British.

The breakthrough for female secretaries came with Churchill's third visit to Washington. Some of them were going too. Experience had shown the disadvantage of employing staff unused to dealing with the papers of high-level committees and the advantages of employing the secretariat's own staff, who were not only used to this work but already knew most of the secrets there were to know. This time Churchill and his entourage were to travel on the liner *Queen Mary,* so the Admiralty could not really object.

Someone who thought that she was not going was Joan Bright. As the most senior woman in the secretariat and one of its most influential figures, she could, on the face of things, hardly object, for her job organising the Special Information Centre seemed an immobile one. But Ismay, as usual, had the answer. 'Would you like to go to Washington?' he began, before asking her to be part of the section under Paymaster-Commander Maurice Knott, which was to organise the administrative arrangements.[11] In Churchill's office Elizabeth Layton screwed up her courage and, knowing that other civilian women were to go, asked close to the time of departure whether she could go too. 'If you wanted to go, why didn't you ask sooner?' was the answer, but go she did.[12]

The exhilaration of those who had for the first time been included in the British delegation, and who boarded *Queen Mary* in the Clyde in May 1943, was understandable. Not only were they going to be at the centre of great events but they were leaving behind shabby wartime Britain for America, where cities had street lights, food was plentiful and the windows of department stores were illuminated, attracting shoppers with goods undreamt of in London that could, moreover, be bought without coupons. The passengers on the great liner were a mixed bunch: the British delegation itself, which numbered seventy, other supporting staff and, kept remote from them, three hundred German prisoners of war, bound for POW camps in the United States. Commander Knott and Joan Bright had their patience tried allocating people to cabins, with the inevitable protests from those who felt their rank entitled them to better accommodation than they had been given. The Cabinet Office and No. 10 Annexe were transposed from the NPO to the ship, with cabins and meeting rooms for the chiefs of staff, Ismay and the Prof, and a suite for the prime minister. In addition to this VIP accommodation, there were twenty-one offices for such bodies as the service departments, Combined Operations, Joint Planning and Intelligence, the typing pool and the Cypher Office, while the industrious Captain Pim set up his Map Room, which Ismay found to be 'as up to date as its counterpart in Great George Street'.[13] During lifeboat drill, Churchill, bellicose as ever, insisted that a machine-gun should be mounted in his boat.

Beneath a veneer of bonhomie, this third Washington Conference saw what diplomats would describe as 'a frank and open exchange of views' and lesser mortals might regard as bitter dissension. The main issues were when to launch an invasion of France, the Americans suspecting that for the British it was really a matter of *if* rather than when, and how much effort should be put into eliminating Italy from the war. Success has many parents, whereas failure is an orphan, and few, after the evident success of the Normandy Landings in June 1944, wanted to be associated with opposition to Operation 'Overlord'. Churchill and Brooke never disagreed in principle with a cross-Channel invasion. However, both were haunted by the experience of the First World War, which had seared Britain (who with her Empire, had lost a million dead) far more seriously than it had bruised the USA. Churchill feared that an invasion might never get beyond the beaches, as had happened at Gallipoli in 1915 (and was to be the case again at Anzio in early 1944), and, even if the landings went well, the penalties of slogging it out toe to toe with the Germans were demonstrated on too many war memorials. This caution apart, there were sound military reasons for doubting the feasibility of invasion in 1942 and 1943, and, even in 1944 a sudden change in the weather or better tactics by the Germans might still have wrecked it. The Americans had no enthusiasm for the British desire to knock Italy out of the war and for the conviction that this would open up further opportunities in the Aegean.

In the end an uneasy compromise was reached. There would indeed be an invasion of France in the spring of 1944 and there was a tacit understanding that this would be after an invasion of the Italian mainland. The price Brooke paid for an American agreement to invade Italy was the withdrawal of significant American and British forces from the Mediterranean area by November 1943 in order to prepare for landings in France. It was not just worries about the inherent military difficulties of invasion and memories of the Somme that made the British so cautious. The essential difference between the British and the Americans was that, while Roosevelt's prime aim was to win the war, Churchill favoured a strategy that would help shape the post-war world. Even in his moments of martial enthusiasm, he was painfully aware that one consequence of a victory which destroyed Germany would be that the old familiar Europe would be changed for ever, and he was left in no doubt that the Americans were not prepared to fight for the restoration of the British Empire.

The Quebec Conference ('Quadrant') came soon afterwards, in August. By then the landings in Sicily had taken place. Joan Bright, becoming indispensable as what she describes as the 'conference house-keeper', went out again to assist with the administration. She had plenty to do, for the delegation was the biggest yet, with 205 members. Allocating cabins, most of which had to be shared, on *Queen Mary*, in order of seniority but with sensitivity towards mutual likes and dislikes, was difficult. Churchill's entourage was as large as ever and he was accompanied by his wife and daughter Mary, but its main working component consisted of John Martin, the principal private secretary, and, as personal secretaries, Patrick Kinna, Geoffrey Green and Elizabeth Layton, the latter now firmly part of the prime ministerial family. Ismay and Jacob led the team from the secretariat which included their personal secretaries.

Both the American and British delegations were installed in the magnificent surroundings of the Château Frontenac Hotel. A constant succession of meetings created a great workload for the Cabinet Office, but the surroundings were spectacular. 'I love this place and we must come here after the war', wrote Jacob, before describing a hectic itinerary:

> At noon, off I went to the Citadel (residence of the Governor General) to meet the PM. At 12.30 p.m. the combined chiefs met, and then again at 5.30. The latter all met the president and the PM again at the Citadel ... They have made very gay here. Every night after dinner a band plays on the promenade, and I believe there is dancing. Miss Wallace [Jacob's secretary] and Co seem to have a pretty good time when they can get off, which isn't often I fear.[14]

Events in the Mediterranean were moving fast as the conference got under way. Fighting was still going on in Sicily, but Mussolini had been forced to resign on 25 July and the new government under Marshal Badoglio was seeking not simply to surrender but actually to change sides. Due to procrastination and inter-allied wrangling over the terms, the opportunity to benefit fully from the Italian surrender was lost. Elizabeth Layton found herself in the midst of this when in

Washington after the Conference she had to awaken Churchill to tell him that 'Some hitch had taken place – the agreement with Italy would not be signed.'[15] She also became privy to one of the great secrets of the twentieth century, the development of the atom bomb, code-named the 'Tube Alloys' project.

The mutual suspicion between the allies continued to be evident at Quebec, with Churchill's desire to reinforce the Italian campaign arousing American fears that he wished to avoid a cross-Channel invasion altogether. Churchill improved relations with the Americans at the expense of his friendship with Brooke when he accepted that there should be an American general (the post eventually went to General Dwight Eisenhower, who had commanded the 'Torch' landings in North Africa) in command of the invasion of France. Considering that the greater proportion of the invasion force, though not of those who made the initial landings, would be American, this was doubtless inevitable. And there was always a risk that the Americans, if they did not get their way, might threaten to go back on their 'Germany first' policy and switch their priorities to the war in the Pacific, but Churchill does not seem to have even tried to get the appointment for Brooke, to whom he had unwisely promised it. The main result of the conference was the confirmation of May 1944 as the target date for 'Overlord' and an expressed aim of defeating Japan within twelve months of the overthrow of Germany.

As yet there had been no meeting of the three allied leaders, and this was now felt to be urgent. Stalin could not be persuaded to travel far from the Soviet Union, and at a preliminary meeting of foreign ministers in

Moscow in October, Teheran was chosen as the venue for the conference. The travel arrangements were far more complex than those for the North American meetings. The main party, headed by the prime minister, left for Alexandria in HMS *Renown*, though some disembarked at Malta and flew on from there. Another group sailed to Alexandria on the heavy cruiser HMS *London*, while others flew the whole way. Joan Bright was again much involved with the preparations and it was now almost automatic that she went to every conference and played a key administrative role.

There was considerable excitement among the War Cabinet secretaries about the possibility of going to conferences. The secretariat was determined that its civilian staff should be well dressed for such occasions and a generous dress allowance and coupons were provided, no mean perks in wartime Britain. Much depended on which senior men were going. Olive Christopher had hoped to go to Moscow for the foreign ministers' conference but Hollis, whose secretary she was, had had to stay behind as Churchill was ill. Ismay had, however, taken along Jacqueline d'Orville, Hollis's other secretary, as well as Betty Green and Mollie Brown, his own secretaries.

Jo Hollis had, up till November, been the one left behind 'to look after the shop' during the 'year of conferences'. The urbane Mountbatten greeted him in Cairo with 'My dear Jo, so they've let you come to a conference at last.' The Cairo and Teheran Conferences were, however, for Hollis, as for Churchill, only the beginning of a long stay abroad, for when he left England on the *Renown* on 12 November, he could not have expected that he was not to return until well into the next year. A cross-section of the secretariat, both military and civil, set off by different modes of transport. With Ismay, Hollis and Burgis on the *Renown* went Olive Christopher, Betty Green and Margaret Fairlie. The ban on civilian women on Royal Navy ships no longer applied. 'Thirty civilian women went from Plymouth to Alexandria on HMS *London*; how far we had gone since Casablanca days!' reflected Joan Bright, who herself set out with the all-the-way-by-air party from Plymouth in what proved to be an uncomfortable series of flights.[16] The staff of the secretariat and No. 10 was ordered to draw up agendas, write the minutes of complex and argumentative meetings or give advice to the prime minister, or to take shorthand notes or wheel out their typewriters in ship's cabins or hotel rooms, calm and efficient as ever. They had to be, for the Americans, deeming Cairo unsafe for a conference, now suggested a change to Malta, where Churchill was breaking his voyage. As usual, the prime minister's own party was considerable: his daughter Sarah, two private secretaries (John Martin and Anthony Montague Brown), Commander Thompson, three personal secretaries (Patrick Kinna, Geoffrey Green and Elizabeth Layton), Sawyers and two detectives. Hollis and Burgis were given the fruitless task of finding accommodation for the president, the most senior of officers and other VIPs in Valetta, a city half-destroyed by ceaseless bombing where even the best hotels or grandest houses now lacked water or electricity. Thankfully, it was decided that, secure or not, Cairo would have to do.

There was still fun and even romance on the voyage: bathing, picnics and trips round the island at Malta, while Olive Christopher had a brief flirtation with a naval officer on *Renown*.[17] In Cairo the Mena House Hotel for the more senior and the Junior Officers' Club for the remainder provided comfort, even luxury, and there were shops with goods unobtainable in London. No sooner was work in Cairo finished than it was off to Teheran, with the delegation travelling in five aircraft.

The two conferences dealt with broadly different areas. Chinese generalissimo Chiang Kai-shek was present at Cairo, where the discussion centred largely on the war against Japan. Stalin was at Teheran, where he obtained agreement on the opening of a second front in May 1944 and the post-war borders of Poland, and committed Russia to attacking Japan after the defeat of Germany. The great sea-change, revealed at Cairo, was the waning of the Anglo-American Alliance, so genuinely beloved of Churchill, as Roosevelt edged away from close cooperation with Britain towards a better understanding with the Soviet Union, and attempted to promote Chiang Kai-shek's China as a fourth great power. Harry Hopkins warned Moran on the way to Teheran that 'You will find us lining up with the Russians.'[18] At Teheran these new divisions seemed to be emphasised by the fact that the British were housed in the British Legation compound and the Americans were not in their own small legation, but in the Russian Embassy. British junior staff, accommodated at the American YMCA with indifferent food and a small stone out-house for washing, found Teheran, with its open sewers, an inhospitable spot. Sir Alexander Cadogan, though more comfortably accommodated, thought it a 'squalid town of bad taste'. Those 'aristocrats among stenographers', as Joan Bright called secretaries Betty Green, Olive

Christopher and Margaret Fairlie, ploughed through the mountains of work that the conference generated. The fact that the meetings got going at all owed much to Ismay using, as ever, his almost miraculous ability to calm troubled waters.

At Teheran the Americans did indeed come close to lining up with the Russians against the British. Both opposed Churchill's plans for the Mediterranean theatre and were infuriated by his refusal to see the May 1944 date for 'Overlord' as set in stone. 'The president promises everything Stalin wants in the way of an attack in the West', grumbled Cadogan in his diary.[19] The conference also saw the western allies agreeing to Stalin's plans for incorporating eastern Poland in the Soviet Union. The appeasement of Russia had begun.

Lord Moran's argument that a loss of mental and physical vigour was responsible for Churchill's lack of success in gaining support for his policies in the last years of the war is probably overstated. It was rather Roosevelt's failing health which contributed to his own poor judgement, enabling Stalin to gain ground. As Norman Brook has written:

> During these months some of the President's senior advisers ... came to believe that there would be better prospects of reaching satisfactory understandings with the Russians if negotiations with them were conducted solely by the Americans without British co-operation. They did not understand, as Churchill had come to realise, what the aspirations of the Soviet Union were for the longer term, and they were deluded by the idea that they could successfully conclude a bilateral deal with the Russians.[20]

These rebuffs to Churchill coincided with a bout of ill-health and made Teheran a miserable conference for him. After further meetings with Roosevelt and Ismet Inonu, president of Turkey, in Cairo, he set off for Tunis, where he was laid low by pneumonia. He was to stay there for nearly a month. Ismay, who had developed bronchitis in Cairo, was on his way back to England and it fell to Hollis, diverted from his voyage home, to go to look after the prime minister in Carthage. Sarah Churchill had been travelling with her father, and Mrs Churchill was sent for but, after several days of deep concern, the prime minister rallied and it was decided that he should eventually go to Marrakesh to convalesce.

To have a prime minister, especially one who exercised such a personal control of the war, ill and distant from London caused major problems in Whitehall. Hollis, once the prime minister seemed out of danger, had to consider what arrangements to put in place and made a quick dash to London and back to arrange the necessary administrative support.

This crisis was to give some of the WAAF officers in the Cabinet Office Cypher Office their first opportunity to leave London. A message from Hollis announced that cypher staff and their equipment were needed in Marrakesh. Naturally the message came via the Cypher Office, and Squadron Officer Williams took the deciphered missive up to Ian Jacob herself, grabbing the opportunity to ask if her unit could go and do the work. Lady Llewellyn, as she is today, describes going to Marrakesh as the 'highlight of the war for the COCO'. She chose officers who had been with the office from the beginning and, after hectic preparations, the party set off on 23 December, along with Hollis, who had promised Churchill he would be back by Christmas Eve, in a Liberator from an airfield in Dorset. At Casablanca, the party split up, Hollis and four of the cypher officers taking off for Carthage, and Joan and the rest going on to Marrakesh.

At Carthage, Hollis was immediately summoned to Churchill's bedroom, for the prime minister had been awaiting his arrival before beginning a meeting with General 'Jumbo' Wilson, Air Chief Marshal Sir Arthur Tedder and Admiral Cunningham. 'Ah, Hollis,' rumbled Churchill from his bed, 'I *knew* you would be back. *Now* we can begin.' Christmas in Carthage and Marrakesh was an exotic interlude, very different from the festival being celebrated in austerity Britain. Attractive young women were in short supply and two of the junior WAAF officers, Ruth Ure and Nora Colville, found themselves having Christmas dinner with Air Chief Marshal Tedder. Wilson and Cunningham joined in the reversal of roles, traditional in the British armed forces on Christmas Day, by serving lunch to the other ranks.

Joan and her party were, meanwhile, settling in at the Mamounia Hotel in Marrakesh. Having just arrived, they were told that there was a dance that evening which they were expected to attend. It was a quaint sort of dance for they were the only women among masses of eager American officers. Christmas Day was spent setting up the Cypher Office in the lodge of the Villa Taylor, where Churchill was to stay. On 27 December Churchill and his party arrived in two planes after a perilous journey over the Atlas Mountains.

A significant slice of the Cabinet Office was now assembled at the Villa Taylor. Jock Colville, who had been summoned back to No. 10 from his service in the RAF, flew out with Mrs Churchill, and both John Martin and Anthony Montague Brown, so three private secretaries were now there. Kathleen Hill, the senior of the personal secretaries, joined Patrick Kinna and Elizabeth Layton. A detachment from the Map Room arrived, as did Hollis's personal and private secretaries, W. R. Jones, Olive Christopher and Brenda Hart. Beaverbrook was there, President Beneš of Czechoslovakia came to lunch, and Generals Eisenhower and Montgomery were visitors. It was almost as if the centre of British government had moved from Whitehall to Marrakesh. By transferring a major part of the NPO team to North Africa, the convalescent prime minister was still 'in complete control of the British Cabinet and war affairs'.[21]

To be transported from winter in Britain to exotic North Africa was an elevating experience for all the party. Elizabeth Layton remembered that 'Ham [Miss Hamblin, another personal secretary] and I really did feel we were in heaven' and romance blossomed for Anthony Montague Brown, who became engaged to a Free French nurse.[22] For the cypher officers, used to being 'back-room girls', this was a sudden translation to life at the top table. 'It is now nearly 60 years since we arrived at Marrakech and memories are fading,' wrote Lady Llewellyn in 2003, 'but all the girls who are with us to-day have two special memories: meeting the Churchill family and being given a tour of Taylor Villa and the wonderful food with white bread at every meal.' Churchill recovered slowly and she remembers him coming back, 'looking cold and tired' from his 'daily trip to the mountains and olive groves'.[23] The cypher officers handled the signals efficiently and received tributes to their work from John Martin and Hollis, now a major-general, for he was promoted while at Marrakesh.

Squadron Officer Williams's detachment returned on HMS *King George V* with Churchill's party. It would provide the communications support at the second Quebec Conference (September 1944), at Churchill's meeting with Stalin in Moscow (October 1944) and at Yalta (January–February 1945) and at Potsdam (July–August 1945).

For the Cabinet Office the first half of 1944 was dominated by preparations for the D-Day landings and the direction of the unyielding slog up Italy. The secrets of the proposed landings had to be closely guarded but were well known to all the secretaries who worked for Ismay, Jacob and Hollis and to many others in the War Cabinet Offices, including of course the planners, intelligence officers and the deception planners whose work on Operation Fortitude (a project which confronted the Germans with phantom landings in both the Pas de Calais and Norway) did so much to make it a success. As Joan Bright recollected, 'Many of us knew the date of "D-Day" from the hour Operation "Overlord" was first mentioned' but the secret was safe with them.

Churchill, as courageous as ever, was only prevented by the direct intervention of King George VI from observing the first wave of the landings from the cruiser HMS *Belfast*. D-Day, 6 June, was preceded by the capture of Rome on 4 June, but Churchill's hope that a successful landing in France would be accompanied by continued American support for his policy of pressing on with the Italian campaign and perhaps advancing on Vienna was firmly rebuffed by Eisenhower and Roosevelt. The promise, so reluctantly prised from Brooke at Quebec in 1943, that seven divisions might, if needed, be transferred from Italy to assist in the invasion of France, was now called upon and the divisions were diverted to landings in the French Riviera (Operation 'Anvil'/'Dragoon'). British influence declined as American forces predominated in increasing numbers. Churchill's plans for the war in the Pacific were also overruled. With the successful establishment of allied forces in France, the continuing erosion of Germany's position in the East and the heavy pounding of German cities, victory was in sight, even if German morale and the extraordinary ability of the German army were alike still underestimated.

By the second Quebec Conference in September, the broad shape of European strategy had largely been decided, and Churchill's proposals for striking through the Ljubljana Gap from north-east Italy and making for Vienna were rejected. The main debate centred on the war against Japan, and the role British forces should play in what was still expected to be a long war in the East.

The British had initially contemplated sending only some twenty-five delegates but eventually fielded their biggest delegation yet, with two hundred and five members, while the Americans brought two hundred and fifty. This time Joan Bright was put in overall charge of administrative arrangements and it was by now firmly established that both the secretarial staff and the cypher clerks of the War Cabinet Office should service conferences. Joan Williams headed a party of nine WAAF officers and Olive Christopher, Sylvia Arnold, Jo Sturdee and Jacquey d'Orville provided secretarial support. Elizabeth Layton found that this second Quebec Conference lacked the 'glitter and magnitude of the first' but that it offered Londoners, used to a dull wartime diet, 'Food of which one sometimes dreamed'.[24]

Churchill, frustrated at what he perceived as America's lack of interest in the map of the postwar world and the interests of Britain on it, now began to ponder whether direct negotiations with Stalin might be the way forward. There was no question of Roosevelt going to Moscow in October 1944, and he had to agree, somewhat reluctantly, to a Churchill–Stalin summit. The British delegation numbered around forty, including Anthony Eden, Field Marshal Sir Alan Brooke (promoted on 1 January 1944) and Ismay, Hollis and Jacob. Joan Bright was again in charge of administration, and the inclusion of all three of the senior members of the secretariat meant that a number of the secretarial staff accompanied them, including Betty Green and Wendy Wallace.

There was by now little Churchill could do for Poland. Wider considerations meant that her frontiers would move inexorably westward, but there still seemed a chance of better terms for the Balkans and central Europe. The so-called 'Percentage Agreement', defining relative influence in post-war Eastern Europe and the Balkans, however, was an exercise in 'Realpolitik' which gave Russia effective control over Romania, Hungary and Bulgaria, the two powers a supposed equality of influence in Yugoslavia, and Britain the decisive say in Greece. Roosevelt was aiming for a new world order based upon the United Nations, but the possibility of the Soviet Union cooperating with that order seemed increasingly unlikely to Churchill. If Greece was, in the long run, the only part of the agreement that Stalin stuck to, this at least helped safeguard British interests in the Mediterranean. The conference was cordial and included convivial banquets and visits to the ballet and opera, and when, as they were leaving Moscow Airport, the British noticed crates of vodka and caviar being loaded onto their plane they felt Russian hospitality had quite excelled itself. It was only after these delicacies had been distributed and consumed back in London that it was discovered they were meant for the Russian Embassy, to which crates of Scotch whisky had to be sent in consolation.[25]

Securing a friendly government in liberated Athens, where fighting had started between government troops and the Communist resistance movement, ELAS, was now a major British aim. Churchill made what was perhaps his most dangerous journey of the war to Athens in December 1944. The British Embassy was under siege and Churchill, the Greek prime minister M. Papendreou, and Archbishop Damaskinos had to withdraw to HMS *Ajax*, where the ship's company were having a Christmas party, to hold a conference. Churchill was shot at outside the Embassy, and his secretary, Elizabeth Layton, found herself in the thick of things, sitting beside the prime minister at a press conference while bullets flew outside and then taking down a letter from him to the ELAS leaders. It was decidedly unlike distant Whitehall. She left on the admiral's barge, sharing a rug with the prime minister as they departed from Athens.

Yalta, in January–February 1945, was the last great wartime conference. For the Cabinet Office the logistics were hugely demanding, with seven hundred and fifty probable travellers: the prime minister was to fly in a Skymaster, and two Yorks were to transport the chiefs of staff and other service officers, while the bulk of the party sailed on the *Franconia*, a converted liner that would act as headquarters ship. There was a brief stop at Malta, where Churchill met Roosevelt, who was aboard the USS *Quincy*, but here the news was received that one of the Yorks transporting middle-ranking staff had ditched in the sea near the island of Lampedusa and all its passengers had been lost. The prime minister and the chiefs flew on to Yalta, but the *Franconia*, disguised as a merchantman, proceeded into the Black Sea through the Dardanelles, controlled by neutral Turkey.

As the ship neared the Crimea injunctions that 'plenty of flea powder and toilet paper [should] be issued to all ranks' did not bode well for the comfort of the passengers bound for the Conference. Joan Bright found herself given the status of major-general in order to get things done, as the Russians were great respecters of rank. The British were put up in the wooden cabins of sanatoria, for the Crimea's benevolent climate made it a favourite spot for fortunate members of the Soviet *apparat* to holiday or recuperate, and hierarchy was tested to its limit as generals sent their batmen to queue for turns at bathrooms and lavatories and a field marshal and air marshal bickered over access to essential conveniences. Yalta was a depressing conference. Churchill was unwell, with a high temperature, and Roosevelt, visibly a very sick man, had only weeks to live. Stalin held all the cards as to the future of Poland and, short of another war, all the British and Americans could do was to trust in the fine words that papered over the fate of this unfortunate country. Churchill had initially expected to enjoy a holiday after the conference but, as soon as it was over, told his staff to get him away from 'this riviera of Hades'.

Victory in Europe Day, Thursday 8 May, did not mean the end of the war, for Japan had still to be defeated. In the CWR, the Map Room walls were now covered with maps of the Pacific and the Japanese home islands. Upstairs in the NPO, staff celebrated with drinks in the canteen and then went up onto the Treasury roof to watch Churchill being applauded by delighted crowds in Parliament Street below. At 3 p.m. they listened to his announcement that hostilities with Germany had ceased. The war in Europe was over, a general election was looming and a grey version of normality was returning to a shabby Britain and a desolate continent.

The Potsdam Conference should have been the grand finale for the victorious Allies and, for the staff of the Cabinet Office and CWR, a time of satisfaction for a victory dearly won, and of looking forward to a post-war future. People were contemplating some sort of normality, planning marriages and thinking about new jobs. The Potsdam Conference was mainly concerned with allied cooperation in the reconstruction of Europe but beneath the surface of agreement for occupied zones of Germany with an Allied Control Commission to coordinate overall policy, tensions were rising. The conference generated a strange atmosphere, a mixture of euphoria, with victory parades and parties amidst the rubble of ruined Berlin, and the depression that became known as Potsdam blues. Many of the British delegation were shocked by the state of Berlin. Joy Milward (now Joy Hunter) a typist in the Cabinet Office, has described 'pathetic groups trudging wearily along in search of wood for fuel, willing to give you anything for some cigarettes or better still a bar of chocolate',[26] and Joan Bright found the smell of Berlin to be that of 'decayed death'.[27]

The war in Europe was over. There was no more bombing, no V1s and V2s, no more agonising about relatives and friends fighting in Africa, Italy or France risking their lives in U-boat-infested waters or on death's short-list in Bomber Command. But there was also a realisation that the most exciting times were over and that the brave new post-war world did not look too promising. For the first time since 1815 Russian troops were in the heart of Europe, tensions between the Soviet Union and the western allies were increasing, austerity and rationing looked set to continue for some time and Britain had emerged from the war, bloodied and unbowed, but manifestly poorer and less powerful.

The Potsdam Conference saw two new Allied leaders. Roosevelt had died on 12 April that year, and his place was taken by Vice-President Harry S. Truman, then unfamiliar outside the USA and not hugely well known even within it. In the midst of the conference Churchill flew home to await the results of the general election. The news that he had been defeated hit the staff of the NPO hard. Few had expected that the man who had been at the centre of their world for so long could actually lose. It was fitting that he was driven from the NPO to Buckingham Palace to resign the great office which he had held with such distinction. Labour leader and deputy prime minister, Clement Attlee, who had accompanied Churchill to the conference, went back to Potsdam in his place with his new foreign secretary, with 'to the astonishment of the Americans and Russians, exactly the same team as had ministered to Churchill and Eden'.[28]

The maps in the CWR were steadily updated until Japan surrendered, and planners continued to work, for it was assumed, until the atom bombs were dropped on Hiroshima and Nagasaki, that the conquest of Japan would take time and cost blood. Upstairs on the second floor Ismay, Hollis and Jacob remained in post. It could not be pretended, however, that there was quite the same sense of urgency now that the street lamps were alight again, and no-one was gruffly demanding 'Action this Day'. On 3 August Ismay told Wing Commander J. Heagerty, a Map Room duty officer, that 'It is very sad to realise that my old friends in the Map Room are leaving one by one, and that what was once a haunt of intense interest and great friendliness will be merely an empty shell.'[29] The CWR were already sliding into the slipstream of history.

6

FROM NERVE CENTRE TO MUSEUM

On 15 August 1945, the day that Japan surrendered, officers on duty in the Map Room ceased work. The closure of the Map Room was marked by no formal ceremony but it was a deeply symbolic moment, for it had been manned twenty-four hours a day throughout the war. Perhaps, as those last duty officers closed the door behind them, they were simply pleased that long shifts underground were over at last. But they may have paused to consider that, on the maps in this room, the whole course of the war, from defeat to victory and from a European conflict to a world war, had been charted day by day. After the defeat of Germany, the protection afforded by the underground rooms had no longer been required and, gradually, much of the accommodation had been vacated by the staff of the secretariat and the chiefs of staff and been converted to more mundane purposes, but the Map Room, the very heart of the CWR, had gone on beating until the very end.

Upstairs in the NPO, the Cabinet Office continued to occupy its wartime space, but there had been a real change of atmosphere after the general election and the replacement of Churchill by Clement Attlee. Though the staff of the Cabinet Office was, at first, little changed, the absence of the charismatic, always demanding and sometimes exasperating, master was felt keenly. Prime Minister Attlee moved briefly into the flat in No. 10 Annexe but soon shifted to No. 10 Downing Street, now once again fully operational.

The WAAF officers continued to run the Cabinet Office Cypher Office for another year before handing it over to civil servants, who required more staff to service it as demarcation lines now prevented cypher personnel from typing the messages, while typists were not allowed to do the cypher work. It says much for the degree to which the high command, although synchronised as one efficient unit, had worked in compartments that, as Lady Llewellyn remembered, when she retired from her post in 1946 and Ismay decided to hold her farewell party in the underground Cabinet Room, it was the first time she had actually been down there.

With the end of the war, the cast of Churchill's inner circle gradually moved on. Lieutenant-General Jacob (soon to be knighted for his war work) left at the end of 1945. He had been a central figure throughout the war and had earned the deepest trust of Churchill. Realising that the peacetime army might not hold out great possibilities for a man who lacked experience of operational command, he began a distinguished career with the BBC.[1] He became director of its European Service, was briefly seconded to the Ministry of Defence when Churchill returned to power in 1951, but went back to the BBC as Director-General in December 1952. He proved a forceful champion of its independence, though his determination to broadcast the truth about the British bombardment of Egypt during the Suez Crisis of 1956 saw the government respond by cutting the budget of the BBC's Overseas Service.

General Ismay stayed in post in the Cabinet Office until November 1946, during a period in which the future organisation of defence was decided, with a new Ministry of Defence controlling (and from 1964 replacing) the old tripartite ministries. He was to have a brilliant post-war career, becoming successively Lord Mountbatten's chief of staff in India, a minister in Churchill's first post-war cabinet and secretary-general of NATO. He was ennobled as Lord Ismay in 1947 and made a Privy Councillor in 1951. Ismay was succeeded as chief staff officer to the Minister of Defence by Jo Hollis, but the nature of that post had changed markedly.

Churchill had been both prime minister and minister for defence, exercising the latter office with the assistance of the secretariat, the chiefs of staff and his own team of advisers. It was now decided that, although the prime minister should retain supreme responsibility for defence, there should be a minister of defence with executive authority and some control over the service departments. Hollis was promoted to lieutenant-general on becoming chief staff officer at the new MOD, a post he held until crowning his career by becoming a full general and commandant-general of the Royal Marines in 1949. The tight link between defence and the Cabinet Office was maintained, as chief staff officer to the new ministry also retained the post of deputy secretary (military) to the Cabinet, but most of what had been the military section of the secretariat staff now moved into the ministry, leaving the accommodation in the NPO, including the War Rooms, to the Cabinet Office. The chiefs of staff system had proved its worth and survived reorganisation, though the three wartime chiefs, Brooke, Cunningham and Portal, retired within a few years of each other, all rewarded with viscountcies rather than the earldoms which went to some successful theatre commanders. Research for this book has reminded me once again of the great debt the nation owes to Brooke, and I am less than ever persuaded that it was properly acknowledged.

The senior civil servants carried on with careers which saw them rise ineluctably up the hierarchy. Sir Edward Bridges became permanent secretary to the Treasury and head of the civil service and was ennobled as Lord Bridges. Norman Brook, who succeeded Bridges as secretary to the Cabinet in 1947, served successive prime ministers and in turn succeeded Bridges as secretary to the Treasury and, like him, became a peer and a privy councillor. Among the private secretaries, Jock Colville became private secretary to Princess Elizabeth, and then returned to Downing Street when Churchill became again prime minister: he was knighted in 1974. John Martin, Churchill's principal private secretary from 1941, became deputy under-secretary at the Colonial Office and then high commissioner to Malta in 1965–67: he too was knighted.

There was only a brief period between the winding down of activity in the CWR and the growth of an appreciation of their historic importance. Most of the unique and top secret documents were removed in November 1947, most rooms were stripped of their original furniture and equipment and were variously converted into conference rooms, a teleprinter centre, a cypher room and a television conference centre for the chiefs of staff. There is now good evidence that a command centre was re-established in the CWR during the Suez Crisis of 1956: an officer told a friend that 'we opened up the CWR for our little war in the Middle East ... we did not touch the old Map Room ... but made another one out of the rooms nearer the mess.'[2] Certain of the more important rooms, including the Map Room and its Annexe, the Cabinet Room, Churchill's office and bedroom and the cubby-hole from which he had made his transatlantic telephone calls to Roosevelt, were left much as they were. There was a growing public awareness of the role the rooms had played during the war, and there were many requests to view them. Lawrence Burgis, the senior Cabinet Office official who had helped set up the rooms in the first place, wrote to Hollis in September 1946:

> I must say I have been astonished at the amount of interest shown in the CWR by the outside public and such like and have always given them every facility to visit the place ... Whether this interest will

> be sustained I cannot say – but I am doubtful. And of course Mr Rance is a marvellous guide, having grown up with the place, and he takes enormous trouble with visitors. Mr Rance is 72 ... but when he is no longer available perhaps some one of our staff (*who knows the place*) and who has reached retiring age, might be kept on as a CWR guide, and perform the other, not too arduous duties now carried out by Rance.
>
> I cannot see the CWR becoming derelict yet awhile. The place is a great standby to me as establishment officer [e.g. officer responsible] for emergency office and sleeping accommodation and I don't know where I should be without it. But you are probably looking farther ahead than the next two or three years during which it will, I am sure, be necessary to keep the place at any rate on the half pay list [e.g. in semi-retirement].[3]

Hollis suggested that a plan should be made for the future of 'these historic premises', saying that he had been impressed by what people had said about the War Rooms:

> For example, Bob Sherwood – a very prominent American author who is at present engaged in writing the biographies of President Roosevelt and Harry Hopkins – said that it would amount almost to a crime against humanity if this place was not kept as a monument to the British higher direction of the war.[4]

By 1948 pressure for public access to the War Rooms was growing and a Conservative MP, Commander

John Maitland, raised the matter in the House of Commons, asking whether the rooms could be kept in their wartime state and the public be allowed to see them. The *Evening News* reported that 'this remarkable underground warren ... is still as it was during the later blitzes.'[5] Those who had helped make its history were now involved in its monumentalisation, for Norman Brook wrote to Sir Eric de Normann, who had played a major role in setting up the War Rooms in the late thirties, agreeing with the proposal to preserve the main rooms on the park frontage, but warning against public access to rooms which formed part of an office where confidential work was carried on.[6] A press conference was held on 17 March at which, after a briefing by Lord Ismay and Mr Rance outlining the plans to preserve the Map Room, the Cabinet Room and the room from which Churchill made his broadcasts, journalists were given a tour of the rooms.

By 1950 Rance's health no longer permitted him to continue as custodian and guide, and General Hollis, now commandant-general of the Royal Marines, was asked if a retired Royal Marine, possibly one who had served in the War Rooms, could be found to take his place. This system, which prevailed during the next decades, was one of the preservation of what were thought the most interesting rooms, with limited access and a custodian/guide to show favoured parties of visitors around. During the seventies and early eighties the custodian was Christian Truter, who regaled the visitors he escorted around the rooms with a wealth of Churchillian anecdotes.

Throughout the 1970s the Cabinet Office and the Department of the Environment, which assumed responsibility for the CWR in 1975, mooted the Rooms' transfer to the Imperial War Museum, but the Museum, heavily committed to other projects (notably its new site at Duxford and the preserved cruiser HMS *Belfast*) had reservations. About 30–40,000 people applied annually to see the rooms but only some 4,500 managed to do so each year, so there was clearly an untapped market. In 1982 the IWM, which had established itself as one of the most innovative and imaginative of major British museums, pioneering interpretative display, the use of modern technology and thematic exhibitions, agreed to take on the CWR. The project was warmly supported by Prime Minister Margaret Thatcher, a great admirer of Churchill, and, despite the economic climate of the time, when schemes for government expenditure were out of favour, the project went ahead: additional money was found which did not detract from the IWM's core funding, and the restored CWR were opened by Mrs Thatcher in 1984.

It was nearly forty years since the end of the war and much of the intimate knowledge of the workings of the CWR had apparently been lost with the deaths of the leading figures. Historians Peter Simkins and Mike Houlihan of the Imperial War Museum, together with Nigel de Lee, who then taught at the Royal Military Academy, Sandhurst, embarked upon extensive research to discover the function and importance of not just those areas, like the Map Room and the Cabinet Room, which had been preserved, but the other parts of the 'underground warren'.

Nigel de Lee's painstaking research formed the basis for the reconstruction, with the Museum's team making decisions on the treatment of historically important rooms and advising on issues such as interpretative text, sound guides and whether or not to have Tussaud-like waxworks or to expose some of the Slab. But there was also an important input from those who had worked down there during the war. Most of the central characters – Churchill himself and Ismay, Hollis, Alanbrooke and Bridges – were dead, though many had left diaries and autobiographies, but there were many relatively senior staff who were very much alive: for instance, both Sir John Colville and Sir John Winnifrith, establishment officer of the War Cabinet Office throughout the war, were still available to help. The more junior officers and, in particular, the secretaries and personal assistants had been much younger than those they worked for. They proved invaluable in charting the history and changing geography of the rooms and, just as importantly, imparting the feeling and atmosphere that had prevailed there.

Jon Wenzel, first curator of the Cabinet War Rooms, has paid tribute to the assistance of the 'girls' whose recollections assisted in the restoration of the Rooms. Joan Bright Astley's book *The Inner Circle* (1971) was a valuable source, and it was reinforced by the advice she gave to the restoration project. She died as this book was going to press, but not before being characteristically helpful to its author. Others who had been at the centre of events in the NPO during the war and contributed to the accuracy of the restoration included Betty Green, Olive Christopher, Jacqueline d'Orville and Wendy Wallace. Further information would be gleaned in future years from secretaries, PAs, stenographers, typists and telephone operators as the museum's reputation increased.

The recreation of a past environment is no easy task, for even everyday items have changed, with plastic often replacing both metal and yesterday's 'modern' material, bakelite. Jon Wenzel found himself collecting items such as wastepaper baskets, chairs, typewriters and other mundane artefacts of office life from the stores of different government departments.

The CWR are redolent of Churchill and of his leadership of Britain during the Second World War, and visitors tend to be as fascinated by the man as by the underground rooms. If they cannot smell the rich smoke from his Havana cigars, they can see the ashtrays and the buckets into which, with great accuracy, he would hurl the stubs, while recordings of his speeches became a central part of the CWR experience. Visitors can see the emergency accommodation provided for him and Mrs Churchill, the Cabinet Room in which he chaired meetings during the Blitz and when V1s and V2s were arriving, the rooms in which he made some of his inspiring broadcasts to the nation, and his phone calls to Roosevelt. The CWR, however, relate to only one period of a long, complex and controversial career reaching from the later years of Queen Victoria's reign to his last premiership in the 1950s, involving changes in political allegiance, high office at an early age but also major setbacks both in war and peace. There was always a case for providing visitors with a broader view of the man who was firmly lodged in the public mind as the greatest Briton of the twentieth century.

In the mid-1990s the Treasury decided that it would vacate what had been the CWR Annexe, some 10,000 square feet of basement into which the underground headquarters had expanded in 1941, but which had been used in recent years as storage space. Phil Reed, who in 1993 had succeeded Jon Wenzel as curator of the CWR, saw a great opportunity. Not only could the existing CWR Museum be enlarged but, adjacent to it, there could be a museum which would be devoted to the life and achievements of Winston Churchill.

Reed's ideas could well have proved a pipe-dream. His parent institution, the Imperial War Museum, lacked the funds for such an ambitious scheme, Whitehall departments had their eye on the space for an underground car park and the project would have to proceed rapidly because it had to be done at the same time as the scheduled redevelopment of the Treasury, which the NPO now housed. The pessimists were confounded, and in 2003 the first stage of the project was completed with the opening of the 'Churchill Suite', the restored rooms which had been set aside for Churchill, his wife and his close advisers. The Churchill Museum was opened by the Queen in January 2005. The whole scheme had cost £14 million.

The combination of Reed's indefatigable enthusiasm, the hard work of the IWM team, the generosity of major donors and the public response in the shape of donations ranging from a few pounds to tens of thousands made the project possible. The large contributions, such as those from the Sainsbury family, the Weston family and the Harmsworths, owners of Associated Newspapers, were essential, but the small donations not only played a significant role but the cheques for £3 or £4 testified to deep affection for Churchill and to his iconic place in the national memory.

The result, the Churchill Museum, created by designers Casson Mann, is a triumphant exposition of

Churchill's life entwined with the history of the time in which he played a major part: it also explores the man's complex personality and foibles. Many museums promise an 'experience', but the Churchill Museum manages to convey one on an interactive table which used sound, words and images to illustrate Churchill's life and times, using technology that helps interpret the significance of documents, letters, paintings and personal possessions, many of them loaned or given by the Churchill family. The treatment is neither hagiographic nor politically correct, and what emerges is close to what many historians would consider to be the state of Churchill's reputation to be today: that of a man of contradictions, whose policies and decisions were often wrong and who had abundant faults as well as shining virtues, but a man with vision, courage and a sense of the broad sweep of historical development.

It is surely apposite that the museum is an integral part of the Cabinet War Rooms, for it was in the darkest days of 1940, when Churchill exercised command of Britain from both above and below ground in Storey's Gate, that courage and determination shone out most brightly, and that many of his faults became virtues. A more rational and calculating man might well have thought that an accommodation with Germany made the best sense in the circumstances, and a less stubborn man, or one less convinced that he had a personal destiny to fulfil, might have lacked the ability to transmit his confidence to a hard-pressed nation.

I have always been drawn to the practice of history by both heart and head. I must have been in the CWR, filming, lecturing or simply rubbernecking (for being a professional historian does not stop me from loving my job) at least fifty times, but there is something about them that takes me back, time and time again. Of course, the process of reconstruction has changed them. The Cabinet Room, for instance, now has a large portal to permit visitors to look into what would once have been a smoke-filled, windowless space. But there are still some of the evocative understains of high command. Few things point up the real importance of the Battle of the Atlantic more sharply than the concentration of holes made in the map by marker pins, a spiking so comprehensive in some areas as to have demanded the insertion of sections of new paper.

Perhaps the British are still inclined to look back at their performance in the Second World War with an overdose of romanticism. Commentators now ponder the morality of the strategic bombing of Germany and Japan, and question the honesty of an alliance with a Russian regime which, as its fellow allies soon knew, had murdered not only tens of thousands of its own citizens but thousands of Polish prisoners of war as well, and observe that the real war was fought on the Eastern Front. Yet it does seem to me that, for all the inefficiencies and inconsistencies inherent in the conduct of operations by a great democracy that had already spent its strength in the First World War, there was something profoundly honourable in the decision to fight on in 1940, long before the United States or the Soviet Union had entered the war. We fought then, not as we might have wished to, but as we had to. I think of the CWR, and that towering figure whose presence is still almost palpable, in the context of the war's first terrible summer, and you must not blame me for feeling proud.

NOTES

Chapter 1: THE STORY BEHIND THE SECRET

1. G. R. Searle, *A New England* (2005), p. 498.
2. Peter Simkins, *Cabinet War Rooms* (1983), p. 12.
3. However, the future Lord Ismay, who had experience of dealing with a colonial uprising in British Somaliland, was sceptical as to the RAF's claims in this respect. *The Memoirs of Lord Ismay* (1960), pp. 34–35.
4. Ismay, *Memoirs*, p. 73.
5. John Charmley, *Churchill. The End of Glory* (1993), p. 306.
6. L. C. Hollis, *One Marine's Tale* (1956), p. 55.
7. Ismay, *Memoirs*, p. 75.
8. John Charmley, *Chamberlain and the Lost Peace* (1989), p. 36, quoting S. Roskill and K. Feiling.
9. Robert Self, *Neville Chamberlain* (2008) p. 238.

10. Harold Macmillan, *Winds of Change* (1966), p. 575.
11. Nigel de Lee, unpublished MS, IWM, p. 1.
12. Ibid, p. 2.
13. Philip Ziegler, *London at War* (1995), p. 337.
14. Malcolm Smith, *Britain and 1940* (2000), p. 26.
15. I am indebted to Richard Bullard, who is writing a dissertation on 'ARP preparations in Oxfordshire 1936–39' as part of an Open University MA in History, for this information.
16. Ziegler, *London at War* pp. 12–13.
17. de Lee, unpublished MS, p. 7.
18. Ibid, p. 23.
19. Hollis, *One Marine's Tale* (1956), pp. 57–58.
20. de Lee, unpublished MS, p. 23.
21. Ziegler, *London at War*, p. 25. This was not wholly correct, for the Treasury was then some distance away.
22. de Lee, unpublished MS, p. 14.
23. Dennis Wheatley, *Stranger than Fiction* (1959), pp. 182–83.

Chapter 2: THE BLAST OF WAR

1. Bill Clavey, BBC, *WW2 People's War*, quoted in Bill Purdue and James Chapman, *The People's War? A Study Guide* (2004), p. 20.
2. Ismay, *Memoirs*, p. 100.
3. John Colville, *The Fringes of Power: Downing Street Diaries 1939–1955* (2004), pp. 19–20.
4. Ismay, *Memoirs*, p. 97
5. Air Vice Marshal William Dickson, IWM Sound Archive, 3168/6.

6. Ismay, *Memoirs,* p. 98. The importance of the secretariat and the quality of its officers are reflected in the progress achieved by these officers, who were successively promoted as the war went on, eventually gaining one-star rank (brigadier and its equivalent) to four-star rank (general and its equivalent).
7. John Vincent, 'Chamberlain, the Liberals and the outbreak of war, 1939', *English Historical Review,* vol. cxiii, no. 451, April 1998, pp. 381–82.
8. Lord Alanbrooke, *War Diaries* (2001), pp.10–11.
9. Robert Rhodes James (Ed) *Chips Channon, The Diaries of Sir Henry Channon* (1967), p. 224.
10. Self, *Neville Chamberlain*, p. 386.
11. Ilene Adams in IWM Sound Archive, 18163/2.
12. This information on staffing of the War Rooms is taken from Nigel de Lee's invaluable unpublished MS in the IWM.
13. Ismay, *Memoirs,* p. 111.
14. Ibid, p. 104. Barratt's plight was complicated by the fact that he was also responsible for the BEF's Tactical Air Component.
15. Paul Addison, *Road to 1945* (1975), pp. 89–90.
16. Colville, *The Fringes of Power*, p. 108.
17. Ismay, *Memoirs*, p. 113.
18. In the last months of 1939 Chamberlain's approval rating reached a peak of 68 per cent and fell back to his peacetime rating in the first quarter of 1940.
19. Colville, *The Fringes of Power,* p. 129.
20. Quoted in Sheila Lawlor, *Churchill and the Politics of War, 1940–1941* (1994), pp. 34–35.

21. See Andrew Roberts, 'The Tories versus Churchill during the "Finest Hour"', in *Eminent Churchillians* (1994), pp. 137–210.
22. John Colville, *The Churchillians* (1981), p. 53. Miss Watson's main responsibility was to advise the prime minister on parliamentary questions.
23. Bracken fulfilled the duties of this post but, according to Colville, firmly refused the title. When Bracken became minister of information, Churchill made no move to find a new PPS but was eventually persuaded to accept George Harvie-Watt MP.
24. Churchill, *Their Finest Hour* (1949), p. 31. The Defence Committee met 40 times in 1940, 76 in 1941, 20 in 1942, 14 in 1943, and 10 in 1944.
25. Quoted in Geoffrey Best, *Churchill. A Study in Greatness* (2003), p. 177.
26. Paul Addison, *Churchill on the Home Front* (1993), p. 334.
27. Sir John Wheeler-Bennett, *Action This Day* (1968), p. 50.
28. He lasted in that post only until July, when he was replaced by General Alan Brooke, later Lord Alanbrooke, who recalled that when he arrived at the headquarters of the Home Forces to take over, Ironside had already gone, leaving a note saying that Brooke could take over the Rolls-Royce he had been using, but 'not a word concerning the defences or his policy of defence etc, absolutely nothing!'. Alanbrooke, *War Diaries*, p. 93.
29. Alanbrooke, *War Diaries,* p. 124.
30. Colville, *The Fringes of Power,* p. 256.

31. Clarissa Eden, *A Memoir: From Churchill to Eden*, ed. Cate Haste (2007), p. 55.
32. de Lee, unpublished MS, p. 55.
33. His suspicions fell on a cousin, a member of the Spanish royal family who was serving in the Italian Air Force, though if, improbably, the attack was indeed a family affair, Prince Christopher of Hesse, who was a Luftwaffe pilot, is the more likely suspect.
34. Colville, pp. 240–41. The name had by now officially changed to Cabinet War Rooms.
35. Ibid, p. 244.
36. Ibid, p. 280.
37. Quoted in Andrew Roberts, *Masters and Commanders* (2008) p. xxxv.
38. de Lee, unpublished MS, p. 68. This survey of Whitehall defence arrangements is based upon this important research.
39. The War Cabinet met in its underground War Room five times in 1942 and only twice in 1943.

Chapter 3: RUNNING THE SHOW

1. James Leasor, *War at the Top* (1959), p. 34.
2. Sir Ian Jacob, IWM Sound Archive, 6191/2.
3. Alanbrooke *Diaries*, 17 Feb. 1941, p. 139.
4. Ibid, pp. 374–5.
5. Elizabeth Nel, *Winston Churchill by his Private Secretary* (2007 edition), p. 9.
6. Gladys Hymer's recollections of life in the CWR, IWM.
7. Ismay, *Memoirs*, pp. 171–2.

8. Jacob, IWM Sound Archive, and Colville, *Downing Street Diary,* 3 November 1940.
9. Joan Bright Astley, *The Inner Circle, A View of War from the Top* (1971), p. 59.
10. Colville, *Downing Street Diaries,* p. 734.
11. Martin Gilbert, *Winston S. Churchill,* vol. 6, p. 594.
12. Colville, *The Churchillians*, p. 132.
13. Joanna Moody, *From Churchill's War Rooms: Letters of a Secretary* (2007), p. 61.
14. After the war a Conservative politician and Cabinet minister (secretary of state for war 1951–6) who became a viscount in 1960.
15. Astley, *The Inner Circle*, p. 88.
16. Best, *Churchill*, p. 176.
17. Alanbrooke, *Diaries,* p. 121.
18. Michael Carver, 'Churchill and the Defence Chiefs', in Robert Blake and William Roger Louis (eds.) *Churchill, An Assessment of His Life in Peace and War* (1996) p. 357.
19. David Fraser, *Alanbrooke* (1987) p. 202.
20. Carver in Blake and Louis, *Churchill*, p. 570.
21. Richard Ollard, 'Churchill and the Navy', in Blake and Louis, *Churchill*, p. 380.
22. Alanbrooke *Diaries*, 26 March 1943, pp. 389–90.
23. Elizabeth Nel, *Winston Churchill* (2007), p. 30.
24. Best, *Churchill* p. 146.
25. Ismay, *Memoirs*, p. 173.
26. Colville, *The Fringes of Power,* p. 398.
27. Channon, Chips: *The Diaries of Sir Henry Channon*, 7 October 1940.
28. Colville, *The Churchillians,* p. 59. Colville adds that the fact that much of this sort of activity came under the Ministry of Economic Warfare, headed

by Dr Hugh Dalton, a man Churchill disliked intensely, doubtless contributed to his lack of interest.
29. F. H. Hinsley, 'Churchill and Special Intelligence', in Blake and Louis (eds)., *Churchill*, p. 408.
30. Colville, *The Churchillians,* p. 59.
31. Henry Pelling, *Winston Churchill* (1974), p. 452.
32. Colville, *The Churchillians,* p. 58.
33. Tom Hickman, *Churchill's Bodyguard* (2008), p. 11.
34. Ibid, p. 104
35. Ibid, p. 109.
36. Randolph and Waugh added a touch of high farce to what is essentially a story of tragedy and betrayal. Waugh mischievously spread the rumour that Tito was really a woman.
37. Richard Hough, *Winston and Clementine* (1990), pp. 504–50.
38. Alanbrooke, *Diaries,* pp. 322–32.
39. Nel, *Winston Churchill*, p. 13.
40. Ibid, pp. 14–15.
41. Winant was unhappily married, and Sarah Churchill's marriage to the comedian Vic Oliver was disintegrating. Randolph and Pamela Churchill were soon to be divorced, and many years later, after his wife's death, Harriman married Pamela. After his death, now an American citizen, she became American Ambassador to France.
42. Walter Reid, *Churchill 1940–45: Under Friendly Fire* (2008), p. 254.
43. Alexander Cadogan *Diaries,* p. 396.
44. Hollis, *One Marine's Tale*, p. 80.
45. Cadogan, *Diaries,* p. 397.

46. Colville attended a viewing of the uncut version at the Ministry of Information and found it 'almost unbearably funny. Lord Cherwell and Inspector Thompson in yachting caps were also mirth giving, not to mention the gestures and twitching of Tommy Thompson who always contrives to be in the forefront of the photographic battle. Nevertheless, the films which lasted over an hour, when suitably bowdlerised should provide a good record of an historic occasion, Colville, *The Fringes of Power*, p. 427.
47. Andrew Roberts, *The Holy Fox* (1997), p. 126.

Chapter 4: LIFE IN THE BUNKER

1. General Jacob said he had never heard the term 'New Public Offices' and that it was always referred to as Great George Street. IWM Sound archive, 6191/2.
2. Ilene Adams, IWM Sound Archive, 18163/2.
3. Moody, *From Churchill's War Rooms: Letters of a secretary 1943–45* (2007), p. 48.
4. Ibid, p. 49.
5. Lady Llewellyn, interviewed by Bill Purdue.
6. This was discovered recently by Andrew Roberts while he was doing research in the Churchill archives at Cambridge. See Roberts, *Masters and Commanders: How Roosevelt, Churchill, Marshall and Alanbrooke won the War in the West.*
7. Information provided by Dr Janet Hunter and Peter Hunter. She was not related to John Colville.

8. Information provided by Alan Heath to the Churchill Museum.
9. Information provided by Mrs Joy Hunter.
10. Astley, *The Inner Circle,* pp. 58–59. Colonel Eddie Combe was head of the Interservices Security Board and he allotted code names for projected operations, such as 'Overlord' for the Normandy invasion.
11. Minutes of Crossbow meeting 15/12/43, National Archive CAB 15/34/21/2.
12. Jacob to Hollis 24/6/43, National Archive CAB 15/34/21/2.
13. Information about the allocation of rooms is taken from Simkins, *Cabinet War Rooms*, pp. 50–54.
14. Roberts, *Masters and Commanders,* (2008), p. 109.
15. Anthony Powell, *The Military Philosophers* (1968), pp. 15–16.
16. Noel Annan, *Changing Enemies* (1995), p. 17, quoted in Michael Barber, *Anthony Powell: A Life* (2004), p. 139.
17. Joan Bright Astley, interviewed by Bill Purdue.
18. Barber, *Anthony Powell,* p. 139. Barber comments that Capel-Dunn's secretarial skills cost him his life, for he was a member of the Cabinet Office team at the signing of the United Nations Charter in June 1945 and was one of the nine passengers presumed killed when their plane disappeared on the flight home.
19. Anthony Powell, *To Keep the Ball Rolling* (1968), p. 158.
20. Ibid, p. 157.
21. Ibid, pp. 158–159.

22. Unlike Powell, Wheatley did not draw upon his experiences in the War Rooms for his novels. His concern for security – he maintained that he was 'stuffed with secrets' – made him cease writing novels set in the present for a time. His wartime experiences are, however, contained in his *Stranger Than Fiction* (1959) and in Volume 3 of his memoirs, *Drink and Ink 1919–77* (1979).
23. Like Powell, he fell out with Capel-Dunn but used his contact with a Higher Authority with whom he used to dine and had Capel-Dunn overruled. He then invited Capel-Dunn to lunch, after which they got on well. Barber, p. 141.
24. Astley, *The Inner Circle*, p. 41.
25. Information supplied by Lady Iliff.
26. Information supplied by Mrs Maxwell.
27. Astley, *The Inner Circle*, p. 89.
28. Churchill, *Their Finest Hour* (1949), p. 541.
29. Moody, *From Churchill's War Rooms*, pp. 59.
30. Astley, *The Inner Circle*, pp. 87–88.
31. Joan Bright Astley, interviewed by Bill Purdue.
32. Mrs Wendy Maxwell, interviewed by Bill Purdue.
33. Mrs Rose Haynes, manuscript, Churchill Museum.
34. Hollis, *One Marine's Tale*, pp. 117–18.

Chapter 5: THE BUNKER GOES ABROAD

1. Philip Warner, *Auchinleck. The Lonely Soldier* (1981), pp. 172–173.
2. Best, *Churchill and War*, p. 120.
3. Colville commented in his diary that it took three cranes to put it into position and would only last for a hundred rounds before its barrel

wore out: the military authorities thought it 'a pure stunt'. *Diaries,* 11 July 1940, p. 189. It was neither the first nor the last Churchillian wonder-weapon to arouse official scepticism.

4. Brian Lavery, *Churchill Goes to War* (2007), p. 283.
5. Lavery gives a detailed account of the travel arrangements for Churchill and his entourage. He casts doubt upon the story that on Churchill's flight home from Bermuda after the Washington Conference in June 1942 the Clipper carrying him passed close to Brest, where German fighters were based. Lavery, *Churchill Goes to War*, pp. 104–110.
6. Roberts, *Masters and Commanders*, p. 339.
7. Astley, *The Inner Circle*, p. 86. We should perhaps have a little sympathy for the Navy's view. In the modern world, with its very different attitude to the relations between the sexes, the Royal Navy has not found the introduction of female officers and ratings into life aboard ship to be without its problems.
8. Nel, *Winston Churchill*, p. 18.
9. Astley, *The Inner Circle*, p. 75
10. I am grateful to Lady Llewellyn for sight of her unpublished recollections.
11. Astley, *The Inner Circle*, p. 90.
12. Nel, *Winston Churchill*, p. 62.
13. Ismay, *Memoirs,* p. 294.
14. General Sir Charles Richardson, *From Churchill's Secret Circle to the BBC. The Biography of Lieutenant-General Sir Ian Jacob* (1991), p. 190.
15. Nel, *Winston Churchill*, p. 76.
16. Astley, *The Inner Circle*, p.102.
17. Moody, *From Churchill's War Rooms,* pp. 74–75.

18. Lord Moran, *Winston Churchill: The Struggle for Survival* (1966), p. 153.
19. Cadogan, *Diaries,* p. 580.
20. Lord Normanbrook, 'Memoir', in Wheeler-Bennett, p. 33.
21. Nel, *Winston Churchill*, p. 87.
22. Ibid, pp. 87 and 88.
23. Unpublished account of the Cabinet Office Cypher Office by Lady Llewellyn, formerly Squadron Officer Williams.
24. Nel, *Winston Churchill*, p. 97.
25. Ismay, *Memoirs*, p. 379.
26. Joy Hunter, typescript lodged with Imperial War Museum.
27. Astley, *The Inner Circle*, p. 219.
28. Colville, *The Fringes of Power,* p.611–612.
29. Ismay to Wing Commander J. Heagerty, 3 August 1945, IWM 94/40/1.

Chapter 6: FROM NERVE CENTRE TO MUSEUM

1. Richardson, *From Churchill's Secret Circle to the BBC,* p. 217.
2. Air Marshal William Dickinson to Wing Commander J. Heagerty, 22 November 1956, IWM 94/40/1.
3. L. Burgis to L. C. Hollis, 4 September 1946, National Archive, CAB 21/4439.
4. L. C. Hollis to L. Burgis, 4 September 1946, National Archive, CAB 21/4439.
5. *Evening News,* 16 February 1948.
6. Norman Brook to Sir E. de Normann, 5 March 1948, National Archive, CAB 21/4439.

ABBREVIATIONS

ATS	Auxiliary Territorial Service
ARP	Air Raid Precautions
BEF	British Expeditionary Force
CID	Committee of Imperial Defence
C in C	Commander in Chief
CIGS	Chief of the Imperial General Staff
COCO	Cabinet Office Cypher Office
COS	Chiefs of Staff
CWR	Cabinet War Rooms
DCOS	Deputy Chiefs of Staff
EPS	Executive Planning Staff
FOPS	Future Operations Staff
GHQ	General Headquarters
HQ	Headquarters
IRA	Irish Republican Army
IWM	Imperial War Museum
JAP	Joint Administrative Planning

JIS	Joint Intelligence Staff
JPS	Joint Planning Staff
LDV	Local Defence Volunteers (later Home Guard)
MIR	Military Intelligence Research
No. 10	10 Downing Street
NCO	Non-commissioned Officer
NPO	New Public Offices
PA	Personal Assistant
PHP	Post-Hostilities Planning
POW	Prisoner of War
SAS	Special Air Service
RAF	Royal Air Force
RAFVR	Royal Air Force Volunteer Reserve
RNVR	Royal Naval Volunteer Reserve
V1	Pilotless Flying Bomb
V2	Long-range Rocket
WAAF	Women's Auxiliary Air Force
WRNS	Women's Royal Naval Service

BIBLIOGRAPHY

Addison, Paul, *The Road to 1945* (1975)
—*Churchill on the Home Front* (1993)
—*Churchill. The Unexpected Hero* (2005)
Alanbrooke, Field Marshal Lord (ed. Alex Danchev and Daniel Todman), *War Diaries 1939–45* (1992)
Annan, Noel, *Changing Enemies* (1995)
Astley, Joan Bright, *The Inner Circle. A View of the War at the Top* (1971)
Barber, Michael, *Anthony Powell: A Life* (2004)
Bellamy, Christopher, *Absolute War* (2007)
Best, Geoffrey, *Churchill. A Study in Greatness* (2001)
Blake, R., and W. Roger Louis (eds.), *Churchill* (1993)
Cadogan, Sir Alexander, *The Diaries of Sir Alexander Cadogan 1938–45* (ed. David Dilkes) (1971)
Channon, Henry, *Chips: The Diaries of Sir Henry Channon* (ed. Robert Rhodes James) (1967)
Charmley, John, *Chamberlain and the Lost Peace* (1989)

—*Churchill: The End of Glory* (1993)
—*Churchill's Grand Alliance. The Anglo-American Special Relationship 1940–57* (1995)
Colville, John, *The Fringes of Power: Downing Street Diaries 1939–55* (1985)
—*The Churchillians* (1981)
Churchill, Winston, *Their Finest Hour* (1949)
Eden, Clarissa, *A Memoir: From Churchill to Eden* (ed. Cate Haste) (2007)
Fraser, David, *Alanbrooke* (1987)
Gilbert, Martin, *Winston S. Churchill*, Vol. 6, *Finest Hour 1939–41* (1983)
—*Winston S. Churchill*, Vol. 7, *Road to Victory 1941–45* (1986)
Hickman, Tom, *Churchill's Bodyguard* (2008)
Hollis, General Sir Leslie, *One Marine's Tale* (1956)
Holmes, Richard, *In the Footsteps of Churchill* (2005)
Hough, Richard, *Winston and Clementine* (1990)
Ismay, General Lord, *Memoirs* (1960)
Jenkins, Roy, *Churchill* (2002)
Keegan, John, *The Second World War (1989)*
Lavery, Brian, *Churchill Goes to War* (2007)
Lawlor, Sheila, *Churchill and the Politics of War* (1994)
Leasor, James, *War at the Top* (1959)
Macmillan, Harold, *Winds of Change 1914–39* (1966)
Moody, Joanna, *From Churchill's War Rooms. Letters of a Secretary 1943–45* (2007)
Moran, Lord, *Winston Churchill: The Struggle for Survival* (1966)
Nel, Elizabeth, *Winston Churchill by his Private Secretary* (2007 ed.)
Parker, R. A. C., *Struggle for Survival. The History of the Second World War* (1989)

Pelling, Henry, *Winston Churchill* (1974)
Powell, Anthony, *The Military Philosophers* (1968)
—*To Keep the Ball Rolling* (1968)
Purdue, A. W., *The Second World War* (1999)
Reid, Walter, *Churchill under Friendly Fire* (2008)
Richardson, General Sir Charles, *From Churchill's Secret Circle to the BBC. The Biography of Lieutenant General Sir Ian Jacob* (1991)
Roberts, Andrew, *Eminent Churchillians* (1994)
—*Masters and Commanders* (2008)
Self, Robert, *Neville Chamberlain* (2008)
Simkins, Peter, *Cabinet War Rooms* (1983)
Smith, Malcolm, *Britain and 1940* (2000)
Vincent, John, 'Chamberlain, the Liberals and the Outbreak of War', *English Historical Review*, vol. 113, no. 451 (1998)
Warner, Philip, *Auchinleck. The Lonely Soldier* (1981)
Waugh, Evelyn, *Sword of Honour* (1965)
Wheatley, Dennis, *Stranger than Fiction* (1959)
—*Drink and Ink* (1979)
Wheeler-Bennett, Sir John (ed.), *Action This Day* (1968)
Ziegler, Philip, *London at War* (1995)

Imperial War Museum, Unpublished Manuscript, Nigel de Lee (c. 1983)

Imperial War Museum Sound Archive:
3168/6 Air Vice Marshal Sir William Dickson
6191/2 Lieutenant-General Sir Ian Jacob
18163/2 Ilene Adams (née Hutchinson)

Recollections lodged with IWM:
Mrs Joy Hunter, Mrs Rose Haynes, Alan Heath and Mrs Gladys Hymers.

National Archives:
CAB, 21/066, 21/2632, 21/5944, 21/4439,
WO 22/434, 28/36

PHOTO CREDITS

1. Winston Churchill and Captain Richard Pym, courtesy of Imperial War Museum (HU 44788)
2. Chiefs of Staff Committee, Getty Images
3. Major-General Hollis, Getty Images
4. General Sir Hastings Ismay, courtesy of Imperial War Museum (MH_027627)
5. General Sir Alan Brooke, courtesy of Imperial War Museum (TR_000149)
6. The dining room in No. 10 Annexe, courtesy of Lady Soames (HU_045907)
7. PM's combined office and bedroom, courtesy of Imperial War Museum (MH_000538)
8. Churchill inspecting bomb damage, courtesy of Imperial War Museum (F 1338)
9. Sandbag pillbox on Birdcage Walk, courtesy of Imperial War Museum (H_001584)
10. Cartoon by David Low, *Evening Standard* 14 May 1940. By permission of Solo Syndication/Associated Newspapers Ltd and the British Cartoon Archive, University of Kent, www.cartoons.ac.uk
11. Government Offices, Great George Street, courtesy of Imperial War Museum (IWM_82_20_177)
12. Concrete apron wall, courtesy of Imperial War Museum (IWM_82_20_180)

13. Telephone, courtesy of Imperial War Museum (IWM_2004_052_0028)
14. G Rance security pass (Misc_81_001232_1)
15. G Rance canteen pass (Misc_81_001232_3)
16. Cabinet War Rooms switchboard, Getty Images
17. 'Careless Talk' cartoon, courtesy of Imperial War Museum (IWM_PST_000731)
18. The 'Dock', courtesy of Imperial War Museum (MH_000533)
19. Mr George Rance and his weather board, courtesy of Imperial War Museum (HU_043777)
20. A Heinkel He !!! bomber over London, 7 September 1940, courtesy of the Imperial War Museum (IWM C 5422)
21. Joan Bright Astley © Joan Bright Astley
22. Ilene Hutchinson, courtesy of the Imperial War Museum (Hutchinson GI_002896_1)
23. Major-General Hollis and colleagues at the Potsdam Conference, courtesy of Imperial War Museum (HU_044888)
24. The 'Big Three', courtesy of Imperial War Museum (A_020711)
25. WAAF Cypher Officers in Marrakesh, by Lady Llewellyn
26. Churchill's birthday, 1943, courtesy of Imperial War Museum (A_020731)
27. The victorious Chiefs of Staff, courtesy of Imperial War Museum (H_41826)

ACKNOWLEDGEMENTS

I particularly thank Bill Purdue for his invaluable assistance across the whole life of this project. Thanks are also due to those who worked in the Cabinet War Rooms and made their recollections available either in writing or in interviews. I am grateful to: Mrs Gladys Hymers, Mrs Rose Haynes, Mrs Joy Hunter, Lady Iliff, Lady Llewellyn, Mrs Wendy Maxwell and the late Mrs Joan Bright Astley. They were all part of the great team of then young women who contributed so much to the smooth running of the command centre of Britain's war. Mr Peter Hunter and Dr Janet Hunter provided information about their mother, Mrs Nora Hunter, and her experiences and Mr Alan Heath contributed his memories of his father's work as an electrician in the War Rooms.

The staff of the Imperial War Museum and Churchill Museum were ever helpful and supportive. Particular thanks are due to Terry Charman, Phil Reed, Abigail Ratcliffe, Cressida Finch, Madeleine James and James Taylor. I have drawn upon documents deposited with the IWM and upon material in its Sound Archive and upon documents in the National Archive. The work of Nigel de Lee who researched the history of the War Rooms for the IWM when it set up the Cabinet War Rooms Museum was an invaluable source as was the book published by the IWM and written by Peter Simkins, *Cabinet War Rooms* (1983).

A book such as *Churchill's Bunker* inevitably rests upon the shoulders of many diaries, autobiographies and biographies as well as many secondary sources but three books must be singled out for their rich portrayals of life in the NPO and within Churchill's entourage: Joan Bright Astley, *The Inner Circle* (1971 and 2007), the vivid recollections of a remarkable woman, who was at the centre of things both in Whitehall and at the major conferences of the Allied Powers; Joanna Moody, *From Churchill's War Rooms. Letter from a secretary 1943–45* (2007) which draws upon Olive Margerison's experiences and provides valuable insights into life in the War Rooms and at the Conferences; and Elizabeth Nel, *Winston Churchill by his Personal Secretary* (1958 and 2007).

INDEX

Index